AF608178

THE CATHOLIC UNIVERSITY OF AMERICA
CANON LAW STUDIES
No. 263

FREQUENT HOLY COMMUNION

A HISTORICAL SYNOPSIS AND A COMMENTARY

by

REVEREND JOSEPH NICHOLAS STADLER, J.C.L.
Priest of the Diocese of San Diego

A DISSERTATION

Submitted to the Faculty of the School of Canon Law of the Catholic University of America in Partial Fulfillment of the Requirements for the Degree of Doctor of Canon Law

THE CATHOLIC UNIVERSITY OF AMERICA PRESS, INC.
WASHNGTON, D. C.
1947

NIHIL OBSTAT:

CLEMENT V. BASTNAGEL, J.U.D.

Censor Deputatus.

Washingtonii, die 14 maii 1947.

IMPRIMATUR:

✠CHARLES FRANCIS BUDDY,

Episcopus Sancti Didaci.

San Diego, die 15 septembris 1947.

PRINTED BY
NEYENESCH PRINTERS, INC.
1801 BROADWAY
SAN DIEGO 2, CALIFORNIA

52

IN GRATITUDE TO
HIS EXCELLENCY,
CHARLES FRANCIS BUDDY
BISHOP OF SAN DIEGO

TABLE OF CONTENTS

CHAPTER IV

CHAPTER V

CHAPTER VI

FOREWORD

FREQUENT and daily Communion is now an established practice among thousands of faithful Catholics. In view of the recent encouragements toward this practice emanating from the Holy See and being spread through the efforts of zealous priests and of pious organizations, there is reason to hope that each ensuing year will see more and more thousands frequently approach the Holy Table to receive the life-giving nourishment of the Blessed Eucharist.

Canonists, and theologians as well, therefore, may find an integrated study of the history and legislation concerning the practice of frequent and daily Communion timely and not without practical value.

The present work is divided into two parts. The first proposes to trace the thread of legislation and custom concerning the frequent reception of Holy Communion from the early days of the Church to the publication of the Code of Canon Law. The second part is concerned with the present legislation connected with the various aspects of frequent Holy Communion as found in the Code of Canon Law and also in the decrees, responses and instructions of the Holy See.

In the early pages of this work references are made to the Fathers of the Church and to other non-canonical sources. This has been done with a view to indicating the practice of the time, in lieu of clear legislation, and is not intended to be exhaustive. Likewise, as legislation became more copious, the present writer found it necessary to confine his consideration to the more outstanding and general enactments. Hence, few particular councils or synods are mentioned in the latter part of Part I.

Part II of this dissertation commences with a broad view of the general obligation to receive Holy Communion and of the various restrictions of law which serve to disqualify certain persons from its reception and to limit its reception for all within the bounds of reason and due respect for this holiest of mysteries.

Toward the end of Part II the field is narrowed considerably, and particular problems are given closer consideration.

The writer wishes to express his gratitude to the Most Reverend Charles Francis Buddy, Bishop of San Diego, for the opportunity of advanced study in Canon Law at the Catholic University of America. Thanks are also gratefully extended to the writer's friends whose thoughtful criticism and help were of undeniable value in the preparation of this work. Finally, the writer wishes to express his deep appreciation to the Faculty of the School of Canon Law for their indispensable assistance in the preparation of this dissertation.

CHAPTER I

EVIDENCE OF FREQUENT COMMUNION FROM THE EARLY CHURCH

Article 1. From the First to the Fourth Century

In the *Acts of the Apostles* it is recorded that the first Christians of Jerusalem "continued steadfastly in the teaching of the apostles and in the communication of the breaking of the bread."[1] There is an indication that the "breaking of the bread" may have been a daily custom with them, for verse 46 of the same chapter reads: "and continuing daily with one accord in the temple, and breaking bread in their houses, they took their food with gladness and simplicity of heart." These passages are generally accepted as references to the reception of Holy Communion.[2] While in themselves they are not conclusive, the tradition of the early Fathers bears indisputable witness to the practice of frequent, if not daily, Communion in the early Church.

St. Justin the Martyr (+ca. 165), who lived in the period immediately after the Apostles, described the custom shaped by the rapidly growing Church. It became customary, he wrote, for all to gather each Sunday for the Holy Sacrifice and the reception of Holy Communion. To each one present a portion of the consecrated bread and wine was distributed, and for those who could not be present, the Sacred Species were intrusted to deacons who brought it to them.[3] The very early *Didache* also indicates that the

[1] Acts, II; 42.

[2] This statement is made in view of the passage's almost inevitable recurrence in treatments on this subject. Some authors, however, dispute whether they rightly apply to the reception of the Holy Eucharist.

[3] Apologia I (ad Antoninum Pium), cc. 65, 67—*Florilegium Patristicum tam veteris quam medii aevi auctores complectens,* (ed. Bernhardus Geyer et Johannes Zellinger: 50 fasciculi, Bonnae: Sumptibus Petri Hanstein, 1911-1940): Fasciculus VII, *Monumenta eucharistica et liturgica vetustissima,* collegit notis et prolegomenis instruxit Johannes Quasten, Pars I, pp. 17-20 (hereafter cited under the name Quasten).

general gatherings of the faithful for the Holy Sacrifice and Communion were for the most part confined to Sundays.[4]

There can be little doubt, however, that the early Christians received Holy Communion as often as they attended the Holy Sacrifice. Passages from Clement of Alexandria (140/50-ca. 215),[5] Origen (185-254),[6] and Tertullian (ca. 160-ca. 240)[7] establish quite conclusively that it was customary for all present at Mass to receive the Holy Eucharist. The apocryphal *Acta Ioannis,* which had their origin about the year 180, mentions explicitly that all present at Mass received a portion of the Eucharist.[8]

There are two canons in the *Canones Apostolorum,*[9] which have given some authors occasion to dispute whether the custom of everyone at Mass receiving Communion was in effect a strict obligation.[10] Canon 8 of this ancient collection enacted a censure of excommunication, or at least of interdict, against those priests, deacons and other clerics who did not communicate at the Mass at

[4]C. 10: "Die autem *dominica,* congregati frangite panem . . ."—Quasten, Pars I, p. 12.

[5]*Stromata,* I, cap. 1, 5, 1.—*Die griechischen christlichen Schriftsteller der ersten drei Jahrhunderte*—herausg. von der Kirchenväter-Kommission der kónigl. preussischen Akademie der Wissenchaften (Leipzig, 1897—), II, 5. Hereafter this work will be referred to as *GCS.*

[6]*Homilia XIII in Exodum—GCS,* VI, 274; Migne, *Patrologiae Cursus Completus, Series Graeca,* (161 vols., Parisiis, 1844-1864), XII, 391 (hereafter cited as *MPG.*)

[7]*De Oratione,* cc. VI, XIX—*Corpus Scriptorum Ecclesiasticorum Latinorum,* ed. consilio et impensis Academiae Litterarum Caesariae Vindobonensis (Vindobonae, 1866—), XX, 184-192 (hereafter cited as *CSEL*); Migne, *Patrologiae Cursus Completus, Series Latina,* (221 vols., 1844-1864), I, 1160, 1182-3 (hereafter cited as *MPL.*)

[8]Acta Ioannis, 86—Quasten, Pars VII, 340.

[9]A collection made in the early fifth century and falsely ascribed to Pope St. Clement I as an addition to the *Constitutiones Apostolorum,* which is a work of the same century. The author of the work is unknown, but it has been demonstrated (cf. Van Hove, *Commentarium Lovaniense in Codicem Iuris Canonici,* Vol. I, Tom. I, *Prolegomena,* 2 ed., Mechliniae: Dessain, 1945, pp. 130-131) that the *Canones Apostolorum* depend upon the *Apostolic Constitutions* and the enactments of the Councils of Antioch, Gangra and Laodicaea for their material.

[10]Cf. Corblet, *Histoire du Sacrement de l'Eucharistie* (2 vols., Bruxelles: Société Générale de Librairie Catholique, 1885), I, 350; also, Dalgairns, *The Holy Communion, its Philosophy, Theology, and Practice,* (6 ed., Dublin: James Duffy & Co. Ltd., 1897), p. 198 (hereafter to be cited *The Holy Communion*).

which they actively assisted.[11] Canon 9 imposed a similar penalty on those members of the laity who left the sacred gathering prematurely without staying to receive Holy Communion.[12]

The words of canon 8, however, quite clearly imply something beyond a simple injunction to receive Holy Communion. There was a warning regarding the possible scandal to the people that could well arise from the neglect of the sacred ministers in this matter. Canon 9, on the other hand, stands unqualified and has been interpreted by some authors as a clear condemnation of those of the faithful who did not receive Holy Communion when present at Mass.[13] This interpretation may seem to gain some support from a letter to the Bishops of Italy, attributed to Pope St. Anacletus (Cletus) (ca. 76-ca. 88).[14] However, this letter has since been proved spurious, having its origin most probably in the pseudo-Isidorian decretals of the ninth century.[15]

In view of Van Hove's opinion that the *Canones Apostolorum* may well have drawn upon the enactments of the Council of Antioch (341),[16] it is likely that the canon under discussion is a corruption of canon 2 of that Council. In it there was a similar directive that those who did not communicate at Mass were to be removed from the church, but only if there were evident signs of vanity or disdain in their abstaining from Communion.[17] A careful comparison of this canon of the Council of Antioch with the words

[11]Bruns, *Canones Apostolorum et Conciliorum Saeculorum IV-VII* (2 vols., Berolini, 1839), I, 2 (hereafter cited *Canones Apostolorum*).

[12]Bruns, *loc. cit.*

[13]Cf. Corblet, *op. cit.*, I, 350, for a more complete treatment of this matter.

[14]*Epistola* I: "Peracta consecratione, omnes communicent; qui noluerint, ecclesiasticis carere liminibus; sic enim apostoli statuerunt, et sancta Romana tenet ecclesia."—Mansi, *Sacrorum Conciliorum Nova et Amplissima Collectio*, (53 vols. in 60, Paris, Arnhem, Leipzig, 1901-1927) I, 602 (hereafter to be cited as Mansi).

[15]Hinschius, *Decretales Pseudo-Isidorianae et Capitula Angilramni* (Lipsiae, 1863), p. 70.

[16]Cf. supra, p. 2 footnote 9.

[17]Bruns, *op. cit.*, I, 81: "Omnes qui ingrediuntur ecclesiam Dei, et scripturas sacras audiunt, nec communicant in oratione cum populo, sed pro quadam intemperantia se a perceptione sanctae communionis avertunt, hi de ecclesia removeantur, quamdiu per confessionem poenitentiae fructus ostendant, et precibus indulgentiam consequantur."

of the *Canones Apostolorum*[18] shows a marked similarity, but also reveals a probable difference of intention in the two canons. The canon of the Council of Antioch seems to state that the act of abstaining from Holy Communion should be accompanied by some signs of vanity or disdain in order to render the subject liable to the prescribed penalty of excommunication. On the other hand, the words of the *Canones Apostolorum* seem to imply that any act of abstaining from Holy Communion was in itself a source of confusion to the church, and, as such, rendered the "offender" subject to the penalty. This is obviously a departure from the intention expressed in the canon of the Council of Antioch and therefore seems to lack a real foundation in law.

It does not seem justifiable, therefore, to conclude on the strength of this doubtful canon, that the custom of everyone receiving Communion at the Mass he attended, in spite of its prevalence, ever became strict law, except perchance in isolated instances.

Up to this point all evidence has indicated that the frequency of Holy Communion among the faithful depended, for the greater part,[19] upon the frequency with which the Holy Sacrifice was offered.

As was seen above,[20] the testimony of St. Justin the Martyr and of the *Didache* seems to indicate that the opportunity of daily Communion was not offered at that early date. St. Epiphanius, Metropolitan of Cyprus (367-403), testified that Wednesday, Saturday and Sunday were set aside by the Apostles as the days on which Mass should be celebrated in order that the faithful might receive

[18]Bruns, *op. cit.*, I, 2: "Quicumque fideles ingrediuntur, et scripturas audiunt, in precatione autem et sacra communione non permanent, ut ecclesiae confusionem afferentes, segregari oportet."

[19]There is evidence that the Consecrated Species were taken by the early Christians to their homes, to be received from their own hands on days when there was to be no Sacrifice of the Mass. However, this does not seem to have been a universally approved custom, but rather was permitted during the times of persecution. See St. Justin the Martyr, *Apologia I* (ad Antoninum Pium) c. 65—Quasten, *op. cit.*, Pars I, p. 17; St. Ambrose, *De Mysteriis*, c. 8—Quasten, Pars III, p. 183; St. Basil, *Epistola XCIII—MPG, XXXII*, 482-486.

[20]*Supra*, p. 1.

Holy Communion.[21] But even this does not seem to have been the universal custom.

The fewness of the churches and of priests in different localities gave rise to a variety of practices. During the first century the Holy Sacrifice was celebrated at Rome only on Sundays; in Egypt, on Saturdays and Sundays; in Cappadocia, and through a great part of Africa toward the end of the third century, on Wednesdays, Fridays, Saturdays and Sundays; at Jerusalem, at Milan, and at the end of the third century in the churches of Italy and Spain, every day of the week. In certain places Mass was celebrated more frequently during the holy seasons of Easter and Pentecost than at other times throughout the year.[22]

Accordingly one cannot speak of *daily* Communion as a universal practice in the early Church with any degree of accuracy; nor can one use the term "frequent Holy Communion" universally[23] for that period, except in a relative sense. For the term as understood today implies the reception of the Most Blessed Sacrament several times a week.

Article 2. From the Fifth to the Ninth Century

With the subsidence of active persecution, and in consequence of the Church's subsequent rapid growth, there arose two factors which tended to bring about a less frequent reception of the Holy Communion among the faithful. In the first place, mass conversions often produced Catholics of lukewarm faith. Constantine's acceptance of Christianity set the vogue for many who espoused the Church for mixed, if not purely selfish, motives. Secondly, and as a consequence upon the first factor, the traditional peni-

[21]*Adversus Haereses,* Lib. III, Tom. II, *Expositio Fidei—MPG,* XLII, 826.

[22]Corblet, *op. cit.,* I, 404.

[23]The word "universally" is purposefully employed here, since there is sufficient evidence that frequent and even daily Communion was practiced in some localities at varying times. Thus, St. Ambrose (+397) in the West strongly urged daily Communion to his flock (*De Sacramentis,* V, c. 4—Quasten, Pars III, pp. 168-169). But at the same time in the East St. John Chrysostom (407) deplored the almost utter neglect of Holy Communion among the faithful (*Homilia V in Epistola I ad Timotheum,* 3—*MPG,* LXII, 529).

tential discipline could no longer be maintained. It had been the common practice to exclude certain classes of penitents from the reception of Holy Communion for long periods of time; and these generally were separated from the main body of the faithful and treated as exceptional to the general rules.[24]

Pastors, confronted with unprecedented numbers of penitents, were unable, from a practical point of view, to confess them all as frequently as necessary, nor could they easily enforce their separation from those who were free to communicate. These circumstances undoubtedly contributed to the eventual supplanting of arduous public penance with secretly performed satisfaction, and very probably to a breakdown of the practice of segregation. As a result, the custom of all the ones present at Mass receiving Holy Communion could scarcely be maintained as strictly as before.[25]

It is at this point in history that the holy writers gave way to vehement exhortations to the faithful, and controversies arose over the dispositions and conditions necessary for the frequent reception of the Holy Eucharist. Evidently universal neglect of the practice had already become prevalent in the East by the end of the fourth century, for St. John Chrysostom complained bitterly of the custom of receiving Holy Communion only once a year. Those who are worthy to receive once a year, he wrote, should be worthy to receive daily; and if they are not, it were better that they abstain even from the annual Communion.[26] St. Augustine (+430), speaking for the West, noted that the practice varied with individuals and localities. "Some," he wrote, "receive the Lord's Body and Blood daily; others, on certain days; elsewhere no day is omitted on which it (the Sacrifice) is offered; in some places only on Saturdays and Sundays, in others on Sundays alone."[27]

[24]Thus in the Council of Elvira (ca. 305), in canons 8, 9, and 69, penalties attached to the sin of adultery included the exclusion from Holy Communion for periods ranging from five years to a lifetime.—Bruns, *Canones Apostolorum,* II, 3, 17.

[25]Cf. Hedley, *The Holy Eucharist* (New York: Longmans, Green & Co., 1907), p. 134; also, Dalgairns, *The Holy Communion,* p. 226.

[26]*De incomprehensibili Dei Natura, Homilia 6, De beato Philogonio*—*MPG,* XLVIII, 755.

[27]*Epistola LIV* (Ianuario, ca. 400), cap. II, n. 2—*MPL,* XXXIII, 200.

While St. Augustine strongly urged frequent, even daily, Communion, he took into account the difficulties and objections of those who urged greater discretion in the receiving of the Sacred Species. Thus, when questioned about the divergence of opinions on the daily reception of Holy Communion, he answered that he neither praised nor criticized the daily communicant, but left it to the individual's conscience and piety to determine which course of action to follow.[28]

Weekly Communion appears to have been practiced by the devout Catholics of that time, and maintained until the beginning of the ninth century.[29] On the other hand, it is clear that some writers and legislators were carried to extremes of rigorism. One curiously rigoristic doctrine in relation to the frequent reception of Communion, which was destined to occupy the thoughts of theologians but tended to confuse the minds of the laity, seems to have been introduced about this period. As early as the end of the fourth century, St. Jerome (+420) proposed that the use of marriage was an impediment to prayer and devotion.[30] About a century later some holy writers were found to urge abstinence from the use of marriage for several days before the reception of the Holy Eucharist.[31] Even the Venerable Bede (+735), while deploring the practice of receiving only three times a year, and exhorting frequent and even daily Communion, made a "measure of continence" a condition of worthiness for married people to receive Holy Communion.[32]

It is impossible to judge the total effect of this undue rigorism, but it was undoubtedly the cause of less frequent Communion for many. It does not seem an unwarranted inference that almost a total neglect of Holy Communion began to take root on an increasingly large scale at this time. For the Council of Agde (506)

[28] *Epistola LIV* (Ianuario, ca. 400), cap. III, n. 2—*MPL*, XXXIII, 201; *Decretum Gratiani*, c. 13, D. II, *de cons.*

[29] Corblet, *op. cit.*, I, 408; Dalgairns, *op. cit.*, p. 226.

[30] *Adversus Iovinianum* (ca. 393), Lib. I, n. 8—*MPL*, XXIII, 220.

[31] E.g., St. Isidore of Seville, *De Ecclesiasticis Officiis*, Lib. I, c. 18—*MPL*, LXXXIII, 756.

[32] *Epistola* II—*MPL*, XCIV, 665.

imposed a strict censure of excommunication upon those Catholics who did not receive Holy Communion on the feasts of the Nativity, of the Resurrection, and of Pentecost.[33]

Yet, whatever may have been the controversies over the dispositions necessary to communicate often, and in spite of the growing neglect of the faithful, the Councils and the Popes continued to urge a more frequent reception of the Most Blessed Sacrament. In the year 747, the II Council of Clovesho enacted that not only children but lay people of all states in life were to be urged more frequently to receive Holy Communion.[34] Another particular Council, held between the years 740 and 750, urged that the reception of Holy Communion should not be put off for as long as a year, as was the custom of many, when the needs of the soul require at least weekly Communion. The Council admonished that the reception of Communion should not be delayed more than three or four weeks, noting that the Catholics of Greece and Rome, as well as of Gaul, received Communion every Sunday.[35] While there is a note of caution in the III Council of Chalon-sur-Saone (813), urging great discretion in the reception of Holy Communion,[36] only a few years later the II Council of Aix-la-Chapelle (Aachen) (836) deplored the omission of weekly Communion and urged the resumption of this holy custom.[37]

The Emperor Charlemagne (+814) even added his great secular authority to that of the Church in urging constancy in the reception of Holy Communion.[38]

[33]Can. 18—Bruns, *Canones Apostolorum,* II, 150; Mansi, VIII, 327; *Decretum Gratiani,* c. 16, D. II, *de cons.*

[34]Can. 23—Mansi, XII, 402.

[35]Councilium Baiuwaricum [sic], can. 6 (740-750, Ratisbon ?)—*Monumenta Germaniae Historica (MGH), Legum Sectio III, Concilia,* Tomus II (Concilia Aevi Karolini), Pars I (ed. Albertus Werminghoff: Hannoverae, Lipsiae, 1904), pp. 51-53, n. 6.

[36]*MGH, Legum Sectio III, Concilia,* Tom. II, Pars I, 283.

[37]Cap. III, can. 22—*MGH, Legum Sectio III, Concilia,* Tom. II, Pars II, 722; Mansi, XIV, 694.

[38]*Capitularia Regum Francorum,* Lib. II, cc. 40, 45 (2 vols., ed. Stephanus Balusius: Parisiis, 1677), I, 750-751. (Reimpressio ex Typis Francisci-Augustini, 1780).

Similar enactments are found in the false *Capitula Benedicti Levitae,* which were added as books V, VI, and VII to the Capitularies of Charlemagne in an effort to introduce measures of reform. The Pseudo-Isidorian decretals, also of this period, contain the forged letter of Pope St. Anacletus (Cletus) mentioned above.[39]

Pope St. Nicholas I (858-867) went so far as to extend permission and encouragement to receive every day in Lent, as well as at any other time throughout the year, to the scarcely civilized and only recently converted Bulgarians.[40]

In view of the foregoing evidence there can be little doubt concerning the Church's desire in the matter of frequent Holy Communion. Yet, because of the danger of abuse and out of respect for the individual's conscience, frequent Communion was not made a matter for strict legislation. In spite of the efforts to the contrary on the part of some would-be reformers, the Church confined itself to exhortations and pleadings. But even these were doomed to be nullified in consequence of the strife that attended the barbarian invasions of the Empire founded by Charlemagne.

ARTICLE 3. FROM THE NINTH CENTURY TO THE COUNCIL OF TRENT (1545-1563)

During the confusion wrought by the barbarian invasions of Western Europe, the practice of frequent Holy Communion fell into almost complete desuetude. This can be explained, perhaps, by the fact that little time could have been left for devotion in the midst of so much physical suffering and privation. But with the subsequent resurgence of Christian life, it may strike the reader as paradoxical that no revival of frequent Communion occurred.

It is true that Pope St. Gregory VII (1073-1085) urged the Countess Malthida to receive Holy Communion frequently,[41] but

[39]*Supra,* p. 3.

[40]*Responsa ad Bulgaras consulta,* art. 9—Mansi, XI, 406; Jaffé, *Regesta Pontificum Romanorum ad annum 1198* (2 ed., curantibus G. Wattenbach, F. Kaltenbrunner, P. Ewald, S. Löwenfeld, 2 vols. in 1, Lipsiae, 1885-1888), n. 2812 (hereafter to be cited as Jaffé).

[41]*Gregorii VII Registrum,* Lib. I-IV, *Epistola XLVII—MGH, Epistolae selectae,* Tom. II, Fasc. I (ed. E. Caspar, Berolini, 1920), pp. 71 ff.

this was purely private counsel. The vast majority of the faithful received but once a year, and this out of respect for the particular councils which demanded it as a minimum. According to Dalgairns (1818-1876), frequent Holy Communion did not exist even among the religious of that time. The nuns of St. Clare received only six times a year; the cloistered nuns of St. Dominic, only four times. The most frequent reception of the Blessed Sacrament seems to have been practiced by the Sisters of St. Mary of Humility,[42] who communicated once every two weeks, and in Lent and Advent every Sunday.[43]

Several Monastic rules, however, between the years 529 (Benedictus, *Regula Monachorum*) and 959 (Dunstanus, Archiepiscopus Cantuariensis, *Regularis concordia*), provided for Holy Communion on Sundays and major feast days, and in some instances, every day of the week.[44]

Aside from stating the obligation to communicate at least once a year, very little legislation on the matter is to be found during this period. The Council of Enham (England) in the year 1009 reiterated the precept of receiving three times a year, but the question of more frequent Communion was not treated.[45]

It would be an over-statement to claim that Gratian (ca. 1140) sought to effect a reform in the neglect of frequent Communion.

[42]Dalgairns probably makes reference here to the sisters of a Monastery of the Blessed Virgin Mary of Humility (Monasterium Humilitatis B. Mariae Virginis), who in the rule were called "Sisters of the Order of Humble Handmaids of the Most Blessed Virgin Mary" (Sorores Ordinis humilium ancillarum Beatissimae Mariae Virginis). This monastery was founded by Isabel of France a little after the middle of the Thirteenth Century. Cf. the article "Isabel of France"—*The Catholic Encyclopedia* (15 vols., and 2 supplements, New York, 1907-1922), VIII, 179 b-c. Cf. also M. Heimbucher, *Die Orden und Kongregationen der Katholischen Kirche* (3. ed., Paderborn: Schoningh, 1933-1934), I, 822-823.

[43]Dalgairns, *The Holy Communion,* pp. 231-232.

[44]Cf. *Textus et Documenta in Usum Exercitationum et Praelectionum Academicarum, Series Theologica,* 16 fasc., Romae: Apud Aedes Pontificial Universitatis Gregorianae, Fasc. 5, *De Frequenti Communione in Ecclesia Occidentali usque ad annum C. 1000,* collegit et notis illustravit Petrus Browe. S.I., (Romae, 1932), pp. 55-60.

[45]Mansi, XIX, 301 (E); Hefele-LeClercq, *Histoire des Conciles* (10 vols. in 19, Paris, 1907-1938) IV, 2me partie, p. 914.

Rather it was his purpose to systematize and harmonize the existing universal and particular legislation of the Church as a means of reform in general. Gratian's choice of sources being somewhat uncritical, his work contains canons from practically every then known collection, for he made no attempt to distinguish between universally authoritative decrees and those of particular or regional councils. And since the Decree of Gratian never received official approval from the Church, it offered no solution to the problem here considered. Nevertheless, the impact of his work was sufficient to lay open the question for the scholars, and to provide them with evidence from the past.

The value of discussing the Decree of Gratian, in so far as the present subject is concerned, lies chiefly in examining the *glossa* or marginal commentaries written by contemporary or immediately subsequent authors. In this way it will be possible to form some judgment on the general attitude and teaching of that time.

Rufinus (+ca. 1190), who in his later life became Bishop of Assisi, wrote the first extensive commentary on the Decree of Gratian between the years 1157 and 1159. Commenting in general on the question of receiving Holy Communion, he summed up what seems to have been the general teaching of his time. One should approach the Blessed Sacrament with great reverence, and if one be married he should abstain from the use of his intimate marital rights for three days before receiving.[46]

Drawing on canon 13, distinction II, *de consecratione*, which canon is there attributed to St. Augustine, Rufinus stated that those who were worthy could receive either more or less frequently, each according to his own belief; not more rarely, however, than the three times a year prescribed by law. Faced with the command attributed to Pope St. Anacletus (Cletus), that all present should receive Communion after the consecration,[47] Rufinus interpreted the Pontiff as speaking only of the three days of precept, that is, the Nativity, Easter and Pentecost. As an alternative interpretation

[46] *Die Summa Decretorum der Magister Rufinus* (ed. H. Singer, Paderborn, 1902), pp. 551-552; c. 21, D. II, *de cons.*

[47] C. 10, D. II, *de cons.*; cf. *supra*, p. 3.

he referred to the reader the commentary on canon 56 of the same distinction, in which the exhortation to receive Holy Communion daily is restricted to priests. The laity, so the gloss as later transcribed by Ioannes Teutonicus (Semeca, +1245), reads, were to receive at the prescribed times, and were to make a *spiritual* communion each day.[48]

The glossator Ioannes Teutonicus, whose commentary appears in the Roman edition of the *Decretum Gratiani,* reflects in general the teaching and the practice of the time. To note but a few facts revealed in his writings: he admitted the practice of more frequent Communion in the early Church;[49] he indicated that the reception of Holy Communion on Holy Thursday was in his day generally observed in the monasteries;[50] that the laity were generally expected to receive three times a year unless they abstained for reasons of humility or in consequence of a state of sin, but were obliged under precept to receive only once a year.[51] He emphasized the necessity of being free from mortal sin for the reception of Holy Communion,[52] and like earlier writers, clung to the idea that married people should not use their intimate marriage rights from three to five days before receiving.[53]

So widespread was the consequent reverential fear and neglect of Holy Communion, that the IV General Council of the Lateran (1215) commanded all, under pain of excommunication, to receive at least once a year.[54] And about one hundred years later, the General Council of Vienne (1311-1312) under Pope Clement V (1305-1314) ordered all clerical monks to receive at least once a month.[55]

[48] *Glossa ordinaria* ad c. 56, D. II, *de cons.*, s.v. *accipere; Glossa ordinaria* ad c. 10, D. II, *de cons.*, s.v. *peracta.*

[49] *Glossa ordinaria* ad c. 10, D. II, *de cons.*, s.v. *peracta.*

[50] *Glossa ordinaria* ad c. 17, D. II, *de cons.*, s.v. *demonstrat.*

[51] *Glossa ordinaria* ad c. 19, D. II, *de cons.*, s.v. *saeculares.*

[52] *Glossa ordinaria* ad c. 24, D. II, *de cons.*, s.v. *qui scelerati.*

[53] *Glossa ordinaria* ad c. 21, D. II, *de cons.*, s.v. *omnis homo.*

[54] Can. 21—Mansi, XXII, 1010; c. 12, X, *de poenitentiis et remissionibus,* V, 38.

[55] C. 1 *de poenitentiis et remissionibus,* V, in Clem.

In view of all this the reader may be led to the opinion that all intimate regard for and devotion to the Most Blessed Sacrament was at a very low ebb during the period from the eleventh to the fourteenth century. Such an opinion is not, however, warranted. This period witnessed a culmination of devotion reflected in the institution of the great feast of *Corpus Christi* by Pope Urban IV in the year 1264.[56] In the bull of institution Pope Urban IV (1261-1264) stressed the greatness of this Sacrament and called upon all to show great reverence and devotion, but nowhere was there an echo of St. John Chrysostom's or of St. Ambrose's call upon all to receive frequently. The clergy and laity alike more and more keenly felt their unworthiness to receive. Hence the repeated warning that no one in mortal sin should receive, and the compromise to make spiritual communions frequently rather than to receive the Body of Christ sacramentally.[57]

[56]*Bullarum Diplomatum et Privilegiorum Sanctorum Romanorum Pontificum Taurinensis Editio* (24 vols. et Appendix, Augustae Taurinorum, 1857-1872), III, 705 (hereafter cited *Bullarium Romanum*).

[57]C. 64, D. II, *de cons.*: "Spiritualiter magis quam corporaliter corpus Christi debemus accipere." Also c? 59, D. II, *de cons.*: "Credere in Jesum Christum, hoc est manducare panem et vinum. Qui credit in eum, manducat . . . Participatione enim filii (quod est per unitatem Corporis Christi et sanguinis) homo manducans vivit, non sumens tantum in sacramento (quod etiam mali faciunt) sed usque ad Spiritus participationem."

CHAPTER II

THE COUNCIL OF TRENT AND THE SIXTEENTH CENTURY

ARTICLE 1. THE COUNCIL OF TRENT

The emergence of the great theological schools of the Middle Ages had served to clarify the issue to the extent of isolating the points of controversy. It became evident that no Catholic writer disagreed on the dogmatic basis for the practice of frequent and daily Communion. That such a practice was pleasing to God and highly recommended by the Church could not be questioned. The controversy turned rather upon the dispositions and conditions required for this frequent reception. It went beyond the question of communicating without thereby committing grave sin, for it was agreed that the state of grace, apart from an advance in virtue or the removal of affection for venial sin, sufficed for a worthy reception of the Holy Eucharist. But for frequent and daily Communion, was this mere absence of mortal sin sufficient? Was not a higher degree of virtue called for? and if so, what degree?

St. Thomas Aquinas (1225-1274) had taught that it was useful and laudable to receive Communion every day if a person should find himself prepared for it. It is evident, however, that the state of preparedness, in the mind of St. Thomas, demanded more than freedom from mortal sin coupled simply with a right intention. For in requiring, on the part of the recipient, that he approach with great devotion and reverence, St. Thomas added that often and in many men (*pluribus hominum*) impediments to this devotion occur on account of an indisposition of the body or the mind, and that it is not useful for all men to approach this sacrament daily.[1] St. Bonaventure (1221-1274) had been even more exacting than St. Thomas, and in conclusion had admitted that the condition of proper dispositions for the daily reception of Holy Communion

[1]*Summa Theologica* (3 ed., Eminentissimo Cardinali Josepho Pecci oblata, 5 vols., Parisiis: Sumptibus P. Lethielleux, 1886; reimpressio, 1923), Pars III, q. 80, art. 10.

was fulfilled in very few (*paucissimus*) cases.[2] It is not surprising, therefore, to find the frequent reception of Communion a rare practice then and in later centuries,[3] in spite of the efforts of some to encourage at least the weekly reception of Holy Communion.[4]

The Council of Trent (1545-1563), while reiterating the Church's desire for a more frequent reception of the Blessed Sacrament, refrained from pronouncing directly on the moral issue of the necessary dispositions for a frequent reception. Only by implication did the Council indicate that persons of average virtue and piety should approach the Eucharistic Table daily. For in expressing an ardent desire "that at each Mass the faithful who are present should communicate, not only in spiritual desire but also by the sacramental partaking of the Eucharist,"[5] the Council made no mention of the more than ordinary sanctity implicitly required by St. Thomas and St. Bonaventure. It may be reasonably assumed that an average congregation would contain very few people in such a state of devotion and preparation; yet the Council's wish was that *all* partake of the Eucharist.

On the other hand, those who supported the more rigorous opinion[6] pointed to another passage of the Council's enactments, which they interpreted as requiring for frequent Communion some other disposition beyond the state of grace and a right intention. The words of the passage are: ". . . that they may believe and venerate these sacred mysteries of His Body and Blood with such

[2]*In IV Libros Sententiarum,* dist. 12, art. 2, q. 2—*Opera Omnia* (10 vols., Quaracchi, 1882-1902), IV, 296, *in fine*: ". . . salva debita praeparatione, quae in paucissimis est ut semper."

[3]St. Francis Borgia (1510-1572) while Viceroy of Catalonia, was publicly criticized as irreverent for receiving Holy Communion every Sunday and feast day. Cf. Ferreres, *The Decree on Daily Communion, an Historical Sketch and Commentary,* translated from the Spanish by H. Jimenez, S.J., (St. Louis; Herder, 1909), p. 36 (hereafter cited *The Decree on Daily Communion*).

[4]Mainly the three Dominicans: Tauler (ca. 1300-1361), Vincent Ferrer (ca. 1350-1419) and Savonarola (1452-1498).—Corblet, *Histoire du Sacrement de l'Eucharistie,* I, 411.

[5]Sess. XXII, *de sacrificio missae,* c. 6. Cf. Schroeder, *Canons and Decrees of the Council of Trent, Original Text with English Translation* (St. Louis: Herder, 1941), p. 147, for the English translation here used.

[6]Cf. *infra,* pp. 19 ff.; cf. also Arnauld, *De la Frequente Communion* (11 ed., Lyons, 1739), cols. 259-262.

constancy and firmness of faith, with such devotion of mind, with such piety and worship, that they may be able to receive frequently that supersubstantial bread . . ."[7] The implication of these words may be understood to mean that a greater than ordinary degree of faith, devotion and piety is required in those who would receive frequently. On the other hand, it is possible to understand the Council as urging these various dispositions not so much as conditions without which Holy Communion may not be received frequently, but rather as motives which impel the recipient to approach the Holy Table frequently.

It is to be noted, too, that the regulations enacted by the Council for the reception of clerics into Minor Orders viewed a more frequent reception of Holy Communion on the part of the candidate as a sign of worthiness of life.[8] While this is not surprising, it is another indication that frequent Communion was even officially regarded as a practice proper to persons who were advanced beyond ordinary degrees of sanctity.

In another passage bishops were instructed to see that seminarians confess their sins at least once a month, and receive the body of our Lord Jesus Christ in accordance with the directions of their confessors. This again left the controversial issue of the conditions necessary for frequent Communion with the moral theologians.

In its legislation concerning regulars and nuns, the Council was content to repeat the regulations of one of the Clementine Decretals,[10] which had directed bishops and other superiors of the monasteries of nuns to take special care that nuns "confess their sins and receive the most holy Eucharist at least once a month."[11]

The Catechism of the Council of Trent (also called the *Roman Catechism*), which was ordered published by a decree of the Coun-

[7]Sess. XIII, *de eucharistia,* c. 8; cf. Schroeder, *op. cit.,* pp. 78-79, and 354-355.

[8]Sess. XXIII, *de ref.,* c. 11.

[10]C. 1, *de statu monachorum vel canonicorum regularium,* III, 10.

[11]Sess. XXV, *de regularibus et monialibus,* c. 10.

cil of Trent[12] and later was issued by Pope St. Pius V (1566-1572), affords an official interpretation of many enactments of the Council.

Regarding the reception of Holy Communion, the Catechism notes that the faithful should not consider the fulfillment of their Paschal duty as sufficient, but should receive Holy Communion oftener (*saepius*). As for whether one should receive every month, every week, or every day, the Catechism states that no certain rule can be prescribed for all. However, it goes on to indicate that the Fathers of the Church, particularly St. Augustine, urged frequent and daily Communion to the faithful. It points out further that it was the practice of Christians of an earlier age in the Church to communicate every day, and that only the cooling of faith and fervor brought about the practice of receiving rarely.[13]

Article 2. Disciplinary Steps

The reluctance of the Council to settle the difficulty by enacting definite rules is clearly explained in a letter from the Sacred Congregation of the Council to the Bishop of Brescia, dated January 24, 1587. The letter reads in part as follows:

> "Although frequent and even daily reception of the most Holy Sacrament has been always approved of by the Fathers of the Church, they never indicated definite rules as to how often in the month or in the week the faithful should abstain from or receive the Holy Eucharist. Likewise, the Council of Trent, no doubt, bearing in mind the infirmity of human nature, while expressing its desire, refrained from giving any prescription on the matter when it said: 'The Sacred Synod desires that all the faithful present at the Holy Sacrifice should partake of the Holy Eucharist.'
>
> "And this has not been done without reason. The manifold recesses of the human conscience and the distractions of those minds which are mostly occupied with the things of this world are veiled from us, and the supernatural gifts which God bestows upon his children are not revealed to human

[12]Sess. XXIV, *de ref.*, c. 7, and sess. XXV, *decretum de indice librorum et catechismo, breviario et missali.*

[13]*Catechismus ex decreto Concilii Tridentini ad Parochos Pii V Pontificis Max. et deinde Clementis XIII iussu editus* (Editio stereotypa, Romae: Marietti, 1930), Lib. IV, *de Eucharistiae Sacramento*, n. 60, pp. 224-225.

eyes; consequently nothing can be pronounced by us as to the worthiness and purity of a soul and its fitness to receive daily the bread of life."[14]

The letter of the Sacred Congregation of the Council just quoted in part was given in response to the Bishop of Brescia, who expressed grave concern over the fact that laymen, "simple people, and even married men, in a word persons whose minds are entirely taken up with the things of this world, are not satisfied with the weekly reception of this sacrament, and dare to receive it every day." Moreover, the bishop noted that in convents grave occasion was given to bickerings and jealousies by the desire of some nuns to receive every day, while others wished to limit their reception of Holy Communion solely to Sundays and festivals.[15]

The bishop therefore proposed a question to the Sacred Congregation, evidently hoping thereby to effect a compromise. The question reads as follows: "May a bishop, in view of the decrees of the Council of Trent, fix some definite days, namely Sundays, Wednesdays, and Fridays, on which alone Holy Communion may be permitted to laymen, married men, and even unmarried women, in order to prevent the abuses which from the daily reception of the Eucharist are likely to follow?"[16]

The Sacred Congregation responded negatively to the query, and stated in effect that any such legislation would defraud the worthy of a divinely given right. The Congregation, while putting the obligation of decision squarely on the individual's confessor, indicated that he is to use great caution and circumspection before he permits daily Communion to ordinary laymen. Confessors and parish priests were urged to insist on the careful preparation required for the reception of Holy Communion, and to bring home, especially to business men and married men, "a profound

[14]*"De la Fréquente Communion"—Analecta Iuris Pontificii,* VII (1864), 782-847, n. 1, Actes de la S. Congregation du Concile en 1587 au sujet de la Communion quotidienne. The English translation of this and the following excerpts from the *Analecta* are taken from Ferreres, *The Decree on Daily Communion.*

[15]*Analecta Iuris Pontificii,* VII (1864), 782-783.

[16]*Ibid.,* col. 783.

knowledge of their unworthiness, a fear of the divine judgments, and a consciousness of the reverence due the Most Holy Eucharist through which Christ is given to us." Furthermore, "those who do not find themselves duly prepared for its reception are to be admonished to abstain."

A special caution was given for married people to "observe continency that they may partake with undefiled souls of this heavenly banquet."

Nuns were to be advised to communicate on the days appointed by the rules of their order. But, "if there are some so conspicuous by purity of conscience or fervor of soul that they are considered worthy of a daily reception of this sacrament, it may be permitted to them by their Superiors."[17]

ARTICLE 3. THEOLOGICAL OPINIONS

In view of the fact that the obligation of directing souls in this matter was officially placed in the hands of the confessor, it may be proper to indicate briefly the opinions of the moral theologians by which the confessors were guided.

Ferreres (1861-1935) has segregated the authors of that time into two camps:[18] the one holding the stricter opinion, as enunciated by St. Thomas and St. Bonaventure,[19] and the other favoring the milder opinion, which later was to receive the official sanction of the Church and to pave the way for the general practice of today. The following paragraphs draw freely from the work of Ferreres.

A. FIRST OPINION

Suarez (1538-1617), after a lengthy and serious treatment of the question, reached the conclusion that "rarely should anyone be advised to communicate, as a general rule, oftener than once a week."[20]

[17]*Analecta Iuris Pontificii,* VII (1864), 789-790.

[18]*The Decree on Daily Communion,* pp. 45-75.

[19]*Supra,* p. 14.

[20]*De Eucharistia,* Disp. LXIX, art. XI, sect. 4, n. 7—*Opera Omnia* (26 vols. in 28, editio nova a Carolo Berton, Paris: Apud Ludovicum Vives, 1856-1868), XXI, 542, *in capite.*

Cardinal de Lugo (1583-1660) reached a similar conclusion expressed in a twofold principle: "First, daily Communion is not suited for all pious souls of every state of life without distinction, nor is it for their greater good, though at times it be not unlawful.

"Secondly, he who does not wish to err in a matter of so great importance, should not be guided by his own judgment; he should stand by the judgment of a prudent confessor or spiritual director, whose office it will be to extend or restrict the frequency of Communion, in view of the greater or lesser fitness of the penitent."[21]

St. Alphonsus Liguori (1696-1787) indicated more precisely in his *Homo Apostolicus* the state of perfection judged necessary for frequent Communion.[22] "In this matter some err through excessive laxity, others through too great rigor. It is wrong without doubt, as our Holy Father Benedict XIV notes in his golden work on the Synod,[23] to allow frequent Communion to such as fall often into mortal sin, or to such as approach Holy Communion with an affection for deliberate venial sin, and with no desire of amendment.

"To certain souls who desire it for their greater growth in the love of God, I judge the director can hardly without scruple deny Communion frequently and even daily, with the exception of one day in the week in accordance with the practice of some directors of experience, and with the exception also of the periods for which they may decide to deprive their penitents of Communion, as a proof of their obedience or humility, or for any other good reason. Such souls, however, should live free from affection for any venial sin, and should moreover be much given to mental prayer and strive towards perfection, no longer falling into sin, even fully deliberate venial sin."

[21]*De Eucharistia*, Disp. XVII, sec. 2, n. 8—*Disputationes Scholasticae et Morales*, (ed. Nova accurante J. B. Fournials, 8 vols., Parisiis, 1868-1891), IV, 156.

[22]Appendix I, § IV *De Frequentia Sacramentorum*, n. 29, (ed. emendatissima, Augustae Taurinorum, Romae: Marietti, 1870), p. 673.

[23]*De Synodo Diocesana* (2 vols., Parmae, 1764), lib. 7, c. 12. n. 9.

Ferreres lists the names of more than forty authors as supporting this stricter view.[24]

B. Second Opinion

Among the first to support the opinion favoring less strict requirements for the frequent reception of Holy Communion was Alphonsus Salmerón (1515-1585), a native of Toledo and an associate of St. Ignatius (1495-1556). Distinguishing three kinds of preparation for Communion, he pointed out that a condign preparation fully adequate to the dignity of the sacrament could be found in Christ alone. A second state of preparation, consisting in a state of high perfection and of a generous practice of virtue accompanied with a deep sense of devotion and reverence, while admirable, was by no means indispensable for frequent Communion; it was ordinarily the fruit of frequent Communion, rather than a preparation for it. The third state, which Salmerón considered necessary but also sufficient for frequent Communion, was freedom from mortal sin, together with the presence of a right intention. His conclusion summed up in a few words the stand of those who favored this lenient opinion:

> "Our conclusion from the foregoing is that neither venial sin, nor dissipation of mind (provided it is not excessive), nor slackness in the practice of virtue, nor the cooling of devotion, meaning by this a loss of sensible fervor, make a man unworthy to approach the Holy Table. For generally all such defects are made up for in the reception of Communion, since it has been instituted for the very purpose of their removal.
>
> "It is good, therefore, to communicate frequently rather than rarely, despite the outcry raised by some writers who by fears and scruples drive men from the tree of life."[25]

Father Cristobal de Madrid, a contemporary of Father Salmerón, was wholeheartedly committed to the same doctrine. In defending his stand, he threw the light of a reasonable interpretation on many passages from the Fathers which might have been

[24]*The Decree on Daily Communion,* p. 51.

[25]*Commentarium in Evangelicam historiam* (Matriti, 1601) tom. 9 in Evang., tr. 42, p. 448, as quoted by Ferreres, *op. cit.,* p. 54.

understood as upholding the stricter view. "If in some of their writings," he wrote, "they seem to make excellence in virtue a necessary condition, it is my opinion that they lay this down, not as indispensable, but as profitable; since the more perfect the dispositions of the communicant, the more readily does our munificent Master pour out His graces. It follows from this that a lack of piety and devotion, and a want of reverence, such as shall not be incompatible with a state of grace, do not make a man unworthy to receive the Sacrament. He may even receive it with fruit and with profit, with this want of reverence and devotion, for the effect of receiving the sacraments frequently is to supply this defect."[26]

The array of authors supporting this opinion, while not as formidable as the number holding the stricter view, is worthy of note. Ferreres cited as supporters of this opinion thirteen Spanish theologians of the sixteenth and seventeenth centuries, although many of these were of only local importance. It is not, however, so much the individual authority of the authors that is to be considered as the contribution made by them as a group. For it is the first clearly defined movement among theologians to break down the rigorism and one-sided view which had become entrenched from the ninth century. It is the first clear-cut emphasis placed on the medicinal and fortifying character of the Holy Eucharist, which is so evident in the common teaching of today.

Article 4. Jansenism

One of the most tragic episodes connected with the history of frequent Holy Communion centered about the ill-conceived and widely propagated doctrine of Cornelius Jansen [Jansenius] (1585-1638) and Du Vergier de Hauranne (1581-1643), Abbe of St. Cyran. As a counter-reform measure to offset the spread of the Massilians, who were Semi-Pelagians,[27] Jansen and St. Cyran sought a return to antiquity through a return to St. Augustine on the

[26] *Monumenta historica* (Matriti, 1896), Vol. IV, p. 9, as quoted by Ferreres, *op. cit.*, p. 59.

[27] Father Alfred, "Some Landmarks of Jansenism"—*The Irish Ecclesiastical Record*, 5th series, V (1915), 449-459.

doctrine of grace and a return to the ancient penitential discipline. Jansen undertook the doctrinal treatise, while St. Cyran, and later Arnauld (1612-1694), elaborated on the moral questions.[28]

Since their doctrine treated all the theoretical and practical questions which pertained to Catholic thought and religious life, it was occupied with the questions of free-will, grace and predestination as well as with the administration of the sacraments, the divers forms of worship and devotion; in a word with Christian practice and its theological foundations.

It is not within the scope of the present work to present a complete analysis of Jansenism. However, in order that the reader may appreciate the problem as something more than a frontal attack on the proponents of frequent Communion, the present writer feels justified in presenting a few of the dogmatic tenets which led the Jansenists to their notorious rigorism.

Jansen, in his single work *Augustinus,*[29] attempted to reconstruct the theology of St. Augustine on the perplexing question of grace and free-will. In so doing he fell into the same errors which had won for Baius (1513-1589), less than a hundred years earlier the condemnation of Pope St. Pius V (1566-1572) in the Bull *Ex omnibus afflictionibus,* of October 1, 1567.[30] Jansen's fundamental error consisted in the opinion that grace and the other prerogatives enjoyed by Adam before original sin were not supernatural, but pertained rather to the integrity of human nature. Hence with the fall of Adam and the consequent loss of these prerogatives, man was essentially wounded in his nature. According to the *Augustinus,*[31] original sin consists in concupiscence, which sets man

[28]Cigno, *Giovanni Andrea Serrao e il Giansenismo nell' Italia Meridionale* (Université de Louvain, Recueil de Travaux, 2e Série, 48e Fascicule, Palermo Scuola Tipografica R. Istituto d'Assistenzo, 1938), p. 215 (hereafter cited *Giansenismo nell' Italia.*)

[29]3 vols., Lovanii, 1640.

[30]*Bullarium Romanum,* VIII, 314; Denzinger, *Enchiridion Symbolorum Definitionum et Declarationum de Rebus Fidei et Morum* (21-23 ed., Friburgi Brisgoviae: Herder & Co., 1937), nn. 1001-1080 (hereafter to be cited as Denzinger).

[31]II, *De statu naturae innocentis,* coll. 74, 106, 158.

in a certain state of accusability (*reatus*) or culpability before God. Even after the remission of this sin, concupiscence remains inseparable from fallen man, and while before sin he habitually tended toward God, to whom he was united by the bond of love, after sin he is turned toward creatures and is no longer able to raise himself toward God by his own strength alone.[32]

The transmission of original sin, moreover, is effected in the descendants of Adam in the midst of concupiscence. This carries with it an unbridled disorder of the sensible appetite, a positive quality which casts man into a vortex of evil.[33] As a consequence, by this same concupiscence, which penetrates man's entire being, man is removed from God and dragged toward the enjoyment of creatures. Here lies the principal font of all our sins. For concupiscence is such that every time it is consented to, with the mere intention of satisfying it, sin is committed, precisely because the love of creatures is a sin in itself.[34] As a result, man can lawfully enjoy God alone, all other pleasures being sinful.

From such a doctrine the step to extreme moral rigorism is indeed a short one. Arnauld, who attempted to defend St. Cyran's extreme views on the reception of Holy Communion, wrote a treatise entitled *Concerning Frequent Communion.*[35] Briefly stated, his practical conclusion was that the soul, befouled with offense and passion, had first to purge itself of its wounds, because in such a state of spiritual illness it could not well assimilate the divine food; only when it had been properly purged could one advantageously approach the Eucharistic Table.[36] There is in Arnauld's work, moreover, an undue emphasis on the recipient's emotions or feelings, which he interprets as proper dispositions for Holy Communion.

Stated negatively, Arnauld's doctrine attempted to disprove four theories of the Jesuit Sesmaisons, who had attacked St. Cyran's

[32]*Augustinus*, II, coll. 185 et seq.

[33]*Ibid.*, col. 210.

[34]*Ibid.*, col. 317.

[35]*De la Fréquente Communion.*

[36]*Ibid.*, p. 692-700.

privately circulated treatise against the practice of frequent Holy Communion. These theories of Sesmaisons are put down in the preface to Arnauld's work: (a) that there never existed in the Church the practice of doing several days of penance before receiving the Eucharist; (b) that to defer Communion does not render the soul more disposed; (c) that to abstain in this spirit does not render more honor to the Sacrament; (d) that even if in ancient times long penances preceded Communion, it would be temerarious to return to that practice at a time when a contrary practice actually existed in the Church.[37]

Conversely, the five errors contained in Arnauld's work are summed up by Brucker as follows:[38] (1) It is in the force of the law and in the prescriptions of Jesus Christ himself, and not through the discipline and institution of the Church, that the order was established according to which "satisfaction" precedes sacramental absolution. (2) With the practice of absolving without delay, the order of penance was inverted. (3) The present practice in administering the sacrament, although supported by the authority of many, and fortified by long usage, is not considered by the Church as an approved practice, but as an abuse. (4) One must consider as sacrilegious those who pretend to have a right to Communion, without first having done penance proportionate to the gravity of their sins. (5) One who does not have a very pure love of God should be deprived of Holy Communion.

It can be said, in conclusion, that in the conception of Arnauld and the Jansenists, Communion was a kind of privilege reserved only to the most perfect; hence, more than an ordinary means of Christian life, it was rather the culmination of a holy life and of an intimate union with God.

To form some idea of the influence of Arnauld's teaching on Holy Communion one has only to glance at the list of contemporaries who gave their approval. Ferreres remarked:[39] "Arnauld's

[37]*Ibid.*, p. 9 of preface.

[38]"Saint-Cyran d'aprés ses lettres inédites (Manuscrit de Munich)"—*Recherches de science religieuse,* IV (1913), 366.

[39]*The Decree on Daily Communion,* p. 81.

work was approved and recommended in the period from 1643 to 1645 by four archbishops, seventeen bishops, and by an entire Provincial Council. Twenty-four further approbations followed from as many doctors of the Sorbonne . . .

"The strangest thing of all is that the four archbishops and as many as ten bishops wrote to Urban VIII a fervent appeal in favor of Arnauld's work, on April 5, 1644. Two other no less laudatory appeals were sent up by the surviving prelates (for some were already dead) to Innocent X on July 21, 1645, and on March 2, 1646, and they sent moreover a delegate to defend the work personally . . . According to these prelates Arnauld's work breathes the spirit of the great saints, and especially of St. Charles Borromeo. 'It is doing,' they declare, 'much good in France, and has led to remarkable conversions not only of sinners but also of calvinistic heretics.' . . ."[40]

Perhaps the foregoing paragraphs contain the explanation why, as Cigno remarks,[41] the Church, in spite of the attacks of Petau (1583-1652), of d'Abra de Raconis (1580-1646) and so many other enemies of Arnauld, never condemned Arnauld's work *Concerning Frequent Communion* to the Index.

The action of the Church against Jansenism was mainly confined to the dogmatic premises whence flowed the moral rigorism. Pope Urban VIII (1623-1644) in the Bull *In eminenti,* on March 6, 1641,[42] forbade the reading of Jansen's *Augustinus* on the grounds that it contained some errors of Baius and also some obscure questions on grace condemned by Pope Pius V (1566-1572) and Pope Gregory XIII (1572-1585) in the previous century.[43]

Later there was a more specific condemnation of five propositions contained in the *Augustinus,* as prepared by Nicholas Cornet

[40]These letters are reproduced in an appendix to Arnauld's *De la Frequente Communion,* pp. 821 ff.

[41]*Giansenismo nell' Italia,* p. 231.

[42]*Bullarium Romanum,* XV, 92 ff.

[43]Denzinger, nn. 1001-1080.

(1572-1663), Syndic of the Faculty of Theology at Paris.[44] This condemnation came on May 31, 1653, in the Bull *Cum occasione* of Pope Innocent X (1644-1655).[45] Arnauld, however, denied that these propositions were to be found in the *Augustinus.* Pope Alexander VII (1655-1667), on October 7, 1656, countered with a definition that they were contained in the *Augustinus,* and presented a formula of submission which Arnauld refused to sign.[46]

The controversy continued under a new champion, Blaise Pascal (1623-1662), during which the strongholds of Jansenism, the convents of Port-Royal-de-Paris and Port-Royal-de-Champs, were suppressed and finally burned. A still more specific condemnation of Jansenistic errors was made by Pope Alexander VIII (1689-1691) in the year 1690.[47]

Among the list of thirty-one condemned propositions are two bearing directly on the reception of Holy Communion: the twenty-second reads: "Sacrilegi sunt iudicandi, qui ius ad Communionem percipiendam praetendunt antequam condignam de delictis suis poenitentiam egerint." The twenty-third: "Similiter arcendi sunt a sacra communione, quibus nondum inest amor Dei purissimus et omnis mixtionis expers."

Although Jansenism in a much altered form was stirred up anew by Pasquier Quesnel (1634-1721) in the early eighteenth century, Pope Clement XI (1700-1721) dealt it a final blow in his Bull *Unigenitus,* published on September 8, 1713, by condemning one hundred and one propositions, many of which were declared to contain the already condemned propositions of Jansenism.[48]

While kind words may perhaps be said for the good intentions of the teachers and followers of Jansenism, for their zeal and purity of life, and for their evidently well-intentioned esteem of the

[44]Alfred, "Some Landmarks of Jansenism"—*The Irish Ecclesiastical Record,* 5th series, V (1915), 454.

[45]*Bullarium Romanum,* XV, 720; Denzinger, nn. 1092-1096.

[46]*Bullarium Romanum,* XVI, 240; Denzinger, n. 1098.

[47]Denzinger, nn. 1291-1321.

[48]Denzinger, nn. 1351-1451.

sacrament of Christ's Body, the well-known effects were little short of catastrophic. Some of their excesses are mentioned by Cigno: "Some, because of those famous 'proportionate dispositions' required by their confessors, abstained from fulfilling their Easter duty,[49] and even in their last agony from receiving Communion in the form of Viaticum, while some priests did not dare ever to celebrate Mass; so it was not a rare case to find among the Jansenists that at the age of thirty some had not yet made their first Communion."[50]

Article 5. Other Extreme Views

In spite of the inroads made by the Jansenists, there were not wanting those who preached and practiced the direct antithesis to their rigorism. Suarez (1548-1617) mentions and refutes an opinion which maintained that everyone attending Mass was obliged to receive Holy Communion at that Mass.[51] Valazquez Pinto is quoted by Ferreres in the following words:[52] "Obedience to divine law obliges us to receive Holy Communion every day, and this doctrine has been expressly taught by St. Jerome, St. Cyril, St. Rupert, St. Bonaventure [!], St. Justin, St. Cyprian, Paschasius, and many other fathers."[53]

It may not be without significance that Pope Innocent XI (1676-1689) in his decree *Cum ad aures,* issued by the Sacred Congregation of the Council during the height of Jansenism in 1679, singled out practices attributable to such extreme views and ordered their speedy correction. The introduction of the decree furnishes a good picture of the abuses that had arisen:

[49]See also Ferreres, *The Decree on Daily Communion,* p. 82.

[50]*Giansenismo nell' Italia,* p. 237.

[51]*De Eucharistia,* Disp. LXIX, art. XI, sect. III, n. 9—*Opera Omnia,* XXI, 537.

[52]*The Decree on Daily Communion,* p. 83.

[53]Ferreres cited many other authors as holding the opinion that it was laudable and lawful to receive Holy Communion on Good Friday and Holy Saturday, viz., Durandus (c. 1275-1334), Sá (1530-1596), Vazquez (1551-1604), Laymann (1574-1635), Hurtado (1575-1646), and others.

"Our most Holy Father and Lord has been informed by the testimony of trustworthy persons that the faithful in some dioceses receive the Eucharist every day, even on Good Friday, and maintain that daily Communion is prescribed by divine law. Likewise, abuses have been introduced in the administration of this sacrament. Some receive the Eucharist at home in their private oratories, or even in bed, though they are not dangerously ill, and they keep for that purpose the Blessed Sacrament in their pockets inclosed in silver pyxes, or ask priests to bring it secretly to them. Others receive several particles at the same time, or hosts of unusual size, and finally many confess their venial faults to priests not approved by the ordinary."[54]

The body of the decree is taken almost *verbatim* from the Congregation's earlier answer to the Bishop of Brescia, briefly accounted for earlier in the present work.[55]

Over and above this corrective measure taken by Pope Innocent XI, there are at least two propositions related to this view condemned by the same pontiff, and one, much later, by Pope Pius VI (1775-1799). The first condemned proposition is to be found in the decree of the Holy Office issued on March 4, 1679. The fifty-sixth condemned proposition reads: "Frequens confessio et communio, etiam in his, qui gentiliter vivunt, est nota praedestinationis."[56] The decree does not give the source of this error, but lists it simply under the title of "Various errors on moral matters." A footnote in Denzinger's *Enchiridion*[57] describes the decree as a condemnation of the moral system called "Laxism."

The second condemned proposition is contained in the decree of the Holy Office of August 28, 1687, and in the Constitution *Coelestis Pastor,* of November 19 of the same year. Both are condemnations of the errors of Miguel de Molinos (1628-1696),

[54]S.C.C., decr. 12 febr., 1679—*Codicis Iuris Canonici Fontes,* cura Emí Petri Card. Gasparri editi (9 vols., Romae [postea Civitate Vaticana]: Typis Polyglottis Vaticanis, 1923-1939. Vols. VII, VIII, et IX cura et studio Emí Iustiniani Card. Serédi.) n. 2848 (hereafter to be cited *Fontes*).

[55]*Supra,* pp. 17-19.

[56]Denzinger, n. 1206.

[57]P. 369.

author and teacher of Quietism. The proposition reads as follows:[58]

> "Nec ante nec post communionem alia requiritur praeparatio aut gratiarum actio (pro istis animabus internis), quam permanentia in solita resignatione passiva; quia modo perfectiore supplet omnes actus virtutum, qui fieri possunt et fiunt in via ordinaria. Et si hac occasione communionis insurgunt motus humiliationis, petitionis aut gratiarum actionis, reprimendi sunt, quoties non dignoscatur, eos esse ex impulsu speciali Dei; alias sunt impulsus naturae nondum mortuae."

The condemnation of the third proposition, issued by Pope Pius VI in his Constitution *Auctorem fidei,* of August 28, 1794, was directed against the errors proposed by the Synod of Pistoia, Italy. The proposition relative to the present subject is number 28, concerning the people's act of partaking of the sacrificial Victim of the Mass. While the proposition bears more directly on the necessity that there be communicants in order to complete the Sacrifice, it indirectly places an obligation of communicating on those who attend.[59]

Some of the above mentioned abuses undoubtedly arose from over-zealous men who, in seeking arguments against Jansenistic rigorism, fell upon examples of extraordinary practices in the early Church.[60] The Church, for her part, while sedulously restraining such exceptions from becoming the rule, condoned the practice of permitting prisoners of the faith to keep the Holy Eucharist with them to receive it by their own hands. This was permitted as late as 1841 to the Christians imprisoned for the faith at Tonkin.[61]

[58]Denzinger, n. 1252.

[59]Denzinger, n. 1528.

[60]Cf. *supra* p. 4, footnote 19.

[61]S.C. de Prop. Fide (C.P. pro Sin.-Tunkin, Occident.), 21 iul. 1841—*Fontes,* n. 4789; *Collectanea S.C. Prop. Fide* (2 vols., Romae: Typographia Polyglotta S.C. de Propaganda Fide, 1907), n. 928 (hereafter to be cited *Collect.*).

More recently a similar privilege was extended to the ordinaries and people of Mexico in consequence of the active persecution of the Church there. Number II, A, of these extraordinary faculties (granted by the S.C. Conc., 23 dec. 1927) permitted the faithful to receive the Most Blessed Eucharist at any hour of the day or night, even without fasting (but if they could foresee the time of Communion they were to fast for one hour before receiving), and to communicate themselves. Number III permitted ordinaries, whenever no suitable and ready priest, deacon, subdeacon, or cleric could be had for administering Holy Viaticum to the sick or dying, to make use of a pious layman who had a common good reputation for his moral character to have him carry the Sacred Species in a vessel, previously to be blessed if it was not already blessed; and the sick person could then receive the Sacred Species with his own hands. If the latter was unwilling or unable so to receive the Sacred Species, They were to be administered by the man who had carried Them, and he was thereupon to wash or purify his hands.—Bouscaren, *The Canon Law Digest* (2 vols., Milwaukee; The Bruce Publishing Company, 1934-1943), II, 26.

CHAPTER III

DEVELOPMENT OF THE PRESENT DISCIPLINE

ARTICLE 1. EARLY RESPONSE OF THE ROMAN CONGREGATIONS

It may be noted, with a degree of admiration, how carefully the Church avoided any and every apodictic settlement of the question during the controversy. Her policy of condemning flagrant abuses on both sides, and of confining her statements to expressions of what was desirable, eventually resulted in a condition amenable to definition. Even after the demise of Jansenism and subsequent to the reforms inculcated through the Decree *Cum ad aures,* almost a hundred years passed without official word on the matter from the Holy See. Yet, the question remained essentially the same as it stood at the opening of the conflict.

Official encouragement toward more frequent Communion, however, is evident from the latter part of the eighteenth century onward. On April 29, 1784, the Sacred Congregation for the Propagation of the Faith, in an Instruction to the Vicar Apostolic of Sutchuen,[1] reproved those "missionaries who, adhering to a too severe practice, turn away from Communion some penitents even after they have confessed and shown a sincere detestation for their sins."

After directing these missionaries to consult the *Roman Catechism* on the matter of preparation for Communion, the Instruction repeated the exhortation of the Council of Trent that all who attend Mass should receive if they are not legitimately impeded. The Sacred Congregation then asked: "How can this be so much as hoped for if only those may receive who are free from the stain of every light fault?" There followed a strong exhortation for the promotion of more frequent Communion, especially for the faithful in China where so many hardships and persecutions made life difficult for them.

[1]*Collect.,* n. 569.

Taking cognizance of the danger in permitting frequent Communion to those addicted to venial sin, the Sacred Congregation stated that it was permissible to use prudently the remedy of medicinal severity on such who may be in the danger of falling into more grave sin. However, this was to be done by way of exception, and not as the rule.

Expressing obvious surprise in noting that the number of confessions far exceeded the number of Communions, the Sacred Congregation listed those penitents who could lawfully be excluded and even repelled according to the rule of the ***Roman Ritual***,[2] but even these were not to be in any way discouraged once they had confessed and made reparation for their sins.

A similar Instruction was issued by the same Congregation in the year 1817 for the missions of China.[3] A part of this Instruction is devoted to the urging of frequent Communion as a source of strength during persecution. Again the hope expressed by the Council of Trent was stressed, and St. Justin (ca. 100-ca. 165)[4] was quoted at length in evidence of the practice of frequent Communion among the early Christians. Finally, the Instruction warned that "Christians are not to be restrained from Holy Communion, but rather exhorted to dispose themselves frequently for Holy Communion through the sacrament of Confession. It is the duty of the sacred ministers to try the spirit of each, to heal the sick, to strengthen the weak, in order that they may worthily approach the Sacred Table." The Sacred Congregation then ordered that "the rules and customs which had been introduced as contrary to these desires of the Church be completely abrogated."

Pope Pius IX (1846-1878) took occasion to emphasize the great value of frequent Communion in two encyclical letters. The first, written on December 5, 1849,[5] referred to more frequent

[2]Tit. IV, cap. 1, *De Sanctissimo Eucharistiae Sacramento,* nn. 8-11.

[3]S.C. de Prop. Fide, instr. (pro Mission. Sin.) a. 1817—*Fontes,* n. 4707; *Collect.,* n. 715.

[4]Cf. *supra,* p. 1.

[5]Pius IX, ep. *Nostis et Nobiscum—Fontes,* n. 508; *Pii IX Pontificis Maximi Acta* (9 vols., Romae, 1856-1878), I, 198-223.

Communion when worthily received as the spiritual food of souls and the antidote by which men are liberated from their daily faults and preserved from mortal sin. The Pope stressed the unifying power of Holy Communion. He called the Eucharist the symbol of that single body of which Christ is the head, to which he wished men, as members, to be united with a most intimate union of faith, hope and charity.

Some years later (1856), in the Encyclical Letter *Singulari quidem,*[6] which was directed against *indifferentism* and *rationalism,* Pius IX urged as an antidote for these evils, among other remedies, that priests encourage the faithful "to both attend the celebration of the divine Sacrifice as frequently as possible with veneration and piety, and to approach the most holy sacraments of Penance and of the Holy Eucharist."

While it may be objected that these are mere exhortations, it must be borne in mind that they are forceful indications of the "mind of the Church." They constitute, in fact, what seems to be a divinely directed preparation for the final action of Pope Pius X (1903-1914). As will be seen shortly from various decrees and papal letters, the laying of this ground work had both an accumulative and a progressive effect.

In 1869 the Sacred Congregation for the Propagation of the Faith issued an Instruction for the missionaries of India.[7] It urged them to instruct most diligently the boys and girls, once they had attained the use of reason, in the strength and dignity of the Holy Eucharist, in order that they might be worthy to become partakers of the divine food in due time. The missionaries were likewise instructed "to assiduously urge the faithful to a frequent use of Confession and Holy Communion."

The next official document pertinent to frequent Communion is to be found in form of a response, under date of December 11, 1885, from the Sacred Congregation of Rites to a query of the

[6]17 mart. 1856—*Fontes,* n. 521; *Pii IX Pontificis Maximi Acta,* II, 510-530.

[7]S.C. de Prop. Fide (C.G.), 12 ian. 1869—*Fontes,* n. 4874; *Collect.,* n. 1340.

Archbishop of Cambrai.[8] The Archbishop's query was presented in form of a doubt: "The said nuns (Moniales a S. Clara, seu Coletinae, e Belgico Regno in Archidioecesi Cameracensi) and some others besides, authorized by their ecclesiastical superiors, received Holy Communion every day, even though according to the rules and decisions of many theologians such a special privilege should be reserved for certain individuals and in certain circumstances only. Since the Sisters would be afflicted with great sorrow if they were deprived of this consolation, the Sacred Congregation is requested to decide what is to be done in the case."

The Sacred Congregation responded, without equivocation, that "the custom is to be praised; and the practice of receiving the Most Holy Eucharist frequently is to be promoted, according to the declarations of the Council of Trent."

Pope Leo XIII (1878-1903) found it necessary, or expedient, to reprove the superiors of many congregations, institutes, and pious sodalities, either of women with simple vows, or of men who according to their constitutions did not take Holy Orders, for going so far as to prescribe by their own authority the days on which their subjects had either to abstain from, or could receive, Holy Communion. This he did in the Decree *Quemadmodum*, issued through the Sacred Congregation for Bishops and Regulars, on December 17, 1890.[9]

Less than a year later the Sacred Congregation for Bishops and Regulars declared, in response to a query submitted by the Bishop of Malaga, that all constitutions prohibiting nuns or men religious from receiving Holy Communion except on certain fixed days were to be considered as abrogated and as having no longer any binding force.[10]

[8]*Fontes,* n. 6170; *Decreta Authentica Congregationis Sacrorum Rituum,* (6 vols., Romae, Typis Polyglottis Vaticanis, 1898-1927) n. 3651. (Hereafter cited *S.R.C. Decreta Authentica.*)

[9]*Fontes,* n. 2017. Pertinent parts of this decree, along with an appropriate commentary, may be found in Part II, pages 105 ff. of the present work.

[10]S.C.Ep. et Reg., *Malacitana,* 14 aug. 1891, ad 3—*Fontes,* n. 2018; Collect., n. 1763.

A further development of this point took place when the Sacred Congregation for Bishops and Regulars established, in article 151 of the directions to be followed in the approval of institutes with simple vows, that any rules appointing certain days on which members of these Congregations have to receive Holy Communion are not to be considered as a refusal to allow them to approach the Holy Table on other days also.[11]

Article 2. Theological Opinions

Seeking a rule for the guidance of confessors in this matter, the Vicar Apostolic of Madagascar submitted to the Sacred Congregation for the Propagation of the Faith the following rules suggested by Father Lehmkuhl (1834-1918) in his *Moral Theology*:

> "It is considered as a necessary condition for frequent Communion (by frequent I mean once or twice a week besides Sundays and feast days) that there be present, first, a serious desire to avoid all deliberate venial sins, so that such faults are of rare occurrence; secondly, an efficient attempt to root out inordinate affections even though not deliberate, and a desire to make progress in virtue; in other words, that there be in evidence a marked advance along the purgative way, and a recognized effort to progress in the illuminative way.
>
> "Daily Communion may be permitted solely to those persons who have not only fought against, but for the most part have also overcome, their inordinate affections, and earnestly aspire to Christian perfection through adjusting their lives to the examples of patience, humility, and poverty of our Lord Jesus Christ, i.e., to those persons who are aflame with the desire to proceed onwards in the illuminative and unitive ways of the spiritual life."[12]

The reply of the Sacred Congregation, dated May 25, 1892, reads as follows: "On careful examination of the scheme proposed by your Lordship, we declare that the rules in question, except the words *not deliberate,* which are perhaps too exacting, may on the

[11] *Normae secundum quas S. Cong. Ep. et Reg. procedere solet in approbandis novis institutis votorum simplicium* (Romae: Typis S. Cong. de Propaganda Fide, 1901), p. 28.

[12] Lehmkuhl, *Theologia Moralis* (2 vols., Friburgi Brisgoviae: Herder, 1883-1884) II, 111-112.

whole be approved, not as absolute law, but rather as directions which may be given to confessors.[13]

The rules suggested by Lehmkuhl constituted the consensus of opinion among the moral theologians in that period. The reader needs only to consult the works of such eminent theologians as Sabetti (1838-1898),[14] Ballerini (1805-1881),[15] Scavini (1790-1869),[16] Gury (1801-1866),[17] and Rosset (1830-1902),[18] in their editions prior to the year 1905, to find almost identical norms.[19]

The only theologian of note in that period to hold an opposite view seems to have been the saintly Father Frassinetti (1803-1868). In his book, *The New Parish Priest's Manual,*[20] he wrote: ". . . notwithstanding daily defects and lighter failings, it is advisable that the faithful should communicate every day." He presented a learned defense of this view in his *Moral Theology.*[21]

The overwhelming majority of moral theologians, then, were inclined to interpret the words of the Council of Trent as an express desire that all Catholics attain a degree of sanctity which would enable them to receive Communion frequently, but at the same time they set up standards and rules far too exacting for the average person.

[13]Cf. Ferreres, *The Decree on Daily Communion,* p. 102.

[14]*Compendium Theologiae Moralis* (3 ed., New York: Pustet, 1888), pp. 485-486.

[15]*Opus Theologicum Morale in Busenbaum medullam* (Prati, 1889-1893), IV, nn. 904-905.

[16]*Theologica Moralis Universa* (11 ed., 4 vols., Mediolani, 1869), III, 129.

[17]*Compendium Theologiae Moralis* (ed. Romana, Romae: 1873), pp. 193-195.

[18]*Theologia Dogmatica-Moralis, De Sanctissimo et Divinissimo Eucharistiae Mysterio* (Camberii: Chatelain, 1876), pp. 474-478.

[19]Ferreres, in his work *The Decree on Daily Communion,* listed the following authors as holding similar views: Marc (+1887), Haine (+1900), Genicot (+1900), Aertnys (+1915), Noldin (+1922), Lahausse (+1928), Gasparri (+1934) and others.

[20]Translation from the Italian by William Hutch, D.D., (2 ed., London: Burns & Oates, 1885), p. 283.

[21]*Compendio della Theologia Morale de S. Alfonso* (2 vols., Genova, 1866), dissert. X, tr. XV, Vol. II, p. 47 ff.

In his Encyclical Letter *Mirae caritatis,* issued on May 28, 1902, Pope Leo XIII spoke strongly and convincingly against this restrictive view:

> "Away with that widespread and pernicious error of those who think the use of the Eucharist should be practically restricted to those who, devoid of care, narrow-mindedly undertake to find repose in a certain plan of a more religious life. For this matter [the reception of the Eucharist], than which nothing is more excellent or salutary, pertains to all alike, regardless of office or dignity, as often as they may wish (and none should not wish) to foster in themselves the life of grace, the completion of which is the attainment of a blessed life with God."

Leo XIII explained at length that the Sacrament of the Eucharist was instituted as a help for all men, a source of faith and the food for men's spiritual life. He pointed out that Christian life flourished in proportion to the frequency with which the Eucharist was received, and languished when it was neglected. His theme may be summed up in a phrase he used often, namely, that the Eucharist existed for the "life of the world." Hence he wrote:

> "We must especially strive to revive the frequent use of the Eucharist among the Catholic laity. The example of the early Church, which we have noted above, recommends it, as do the decrees of the Councils and the authority of the Fathers and the most holy men of every age; for as the body requires food frequently, so too does the soul; and the most holy Eucharist affords us this most life-giving nourishment. And so the prejudiced opinions of the adversaries, the senseless fears of many, and the specious arguments for abstaining are to be thoroughly rooted out; for it concerns a matter than which nothing is more useful to the faithful for freeing them from the disquieting cares of temporal matters, and for reclaiming and steadfastly preserving Christian souls. Hence of great importance will be the zeal and the solicitude of the clergy. For priests, to whom Christ the Redeemer has entrusted the office of effecting and distributing the mysteries of His Body and Blood, can make return for this greatest of honors in no better way than by zealously promoting His Eucharistic

glory, and in fulfilling the wishes of His most Sacred Heart, invite and draw the souls of men to the health-bringing fonts of this great Sacrament and Sacrifice."[22]

These forceful words of Pope Leo XIII were the last to be spoken by way of preparation for the definitive decree of Pope Pius X. It has been noted that the correction of abuses and the urgent appeals on the part of the Holy See were not sufficient to dispel the confusion of confessors, or to inflame theologians universally for championing the cause of a more widespread frequent reception of Holy Communion. It required more than exhortations to cause conservative moralists to abandon the unmistakable teaching of St. Bonaventure and St. Alphonsus.[23]

ARTICLE 3. DECREE OF POPE PIUS X

The Decree *Sacra Tridentina Synodus* of Pope Pius X was issued through the Sacred Congregation of the Council on December 20, 1905.[24] Inasmuch as it settles once and for all the long standing controversy in a remarkably clear and simple manner, and for the reason that it remains in force today as a norm prescribed by the *Code of Canon Law*,[25] it merits special consideration.

The decree is aptly divided into two parts: the first is dogmatic and historical in its character, and the second is disciplinary. In view of the fact that the present study has developed at length the historical background of the question, there can be little advantage in repeating this part of the decree.

The disciplinary part of the decree consists of nine articles. These articles are so clear and precise that the present writer feels that any rewording would detract from rather than add to the easy understanding of them. Hence they are reproduced here according to the translation originally furnished in the *London Tablet*.[26]

[22]N. 11—*Fontes*, n. 648; *Leonis XIII Pontificis Maximi Acta* (23 vols., Romae, 1881-1905), XXII, 135-136.

[23]St. Alphonsus Liguori, *Theologia Moralis* (9 vols., Taurini: Marietti, 1827), II, 147; also, *Praxis Confessarii ad bene Excipiendas Confessiones* (Parisiis: Apud A. Leclere, 1804), Cap. IX, § IV, pp. 220 ff.

[24]*Fontes*, n. 4326; *Collect.*, n. 2225.

[25]Can. 863.

[26]As reproduced in Ferreres, *The Decree on Daily Communion*, pp. 24 ff.

1. "Frequent and daily Communion, as a thing most earnestly desired by Christ Our Lord and by the Catholic Church should be open to all the faithful, of whatever rank and condition of life; so that no one who is in a state of grace, and who approaches the holy table with a right and devout intention, can lawfully be hindered therefrom.

2. "A right intention consists in this: that he who approaches the holy table should do so, not out of routine or vainglory or human respect, but for the purpose of pleasing God, of being more closely united with Him by charity, and of seeking this divine remedy for his weaknesses and defects.

3. "Although it is most expedient that those who communicate frequently or daily should be free from venial sins, especially from such as are fully deliberate, and from any affection thereto; nevertheless, it is sufficient that they be free from mortal sin, with the purpose of never sinning mortally in the future; and if they have this sincere purpose, it is impossible but that daily communicants should gradually emancipate themselves from even venial sins, and from all affection thereto.

4. "But whereas the Sacraments of the New Law, though they take effect *ex opere operato,* nevertheless produce a greater effect in proportion as the dispositions of the recipient are better; therefore, care is to be taken that Holy Communion be preceded by serious preparation, and followed by a suitable thanksgiving according to each one's strength, circumstances, and duties.

5. "That the practice of frequent and daily Communion may be carried out with greater prudence and more abundant merit, the confessor's advice should be asked. Confessors, however, are to be careful not to dissuade anyone (*ne quemquam avertant*) from frequent and daily Communion, provided that he is in a state of grace, and approaches with a right intention.

6. "But since it is plain that, by the frequent or daily reception of the Holy Eucharist, union with Christ is fostered, the spiritual life more abundantly sustained, the soul more richly endowed with virtues, and an even surer pledge of everlasting happiness bestowed on the recipient; therefore parish priests, confessors, and preachers — in accordance with the approved teaching of the Roman Catechism (Part II, cap. 4, n. 63)—are frequently, and with great zeal, to exhort the faithful to this devout and salutary practice.

7. "Frequent and daily Communion is to be promoted especially in religious orders and congregations of all kinds; with regard to which, however, the decree '*Quemadmodum*,' issued on December 17, 1890, by the Sacred Congregation of Bishops and Regulars is to remain in force. It is also to be promoted especially in ecclesiastical seminaries, where students are preparing for the service of the altar; as also in all Christian establishments, of whatever kind, for the training of youth.

8. "In the case of religious institutes, whether of solemn or simple vows, in whose rules, or constitutions, or calendars, Communion is assigned to certain fixed days, such regulations are to be regarded as *directive* and not *preceptive.* In such cases the appointed number of Communions should be regarded as a minimum, and not as setting a limit to the devotion of the religious. Therefore, freedom of access to the Eucharistic table, whether more frequently or daily, must always be allowed them, according to the principles above laid down in this decree. And in order that all religious of both sexes may clearly understand the provisions of this decree, the superior of each house is to see that it is read in the community, in the vernacular, every year, within the octave of the Feast of Corpus Christi.

9. "Finally, after the publication of this decree, all ecclesiastical writers are to cease from contentious controversies concerning the dispositions requisite for frequent and daily Communion.

"All this having been reported to His Holiness Pope Pius X by the undersigned secretary of the Sacred Congregation, in an audience held on December 17, 1905, His Holiness ratified and confirmed the present decree, and ordered it to be published, anything to the contrary notwithstanding. He further ordered that it should be sent to all local ordinaries and regular prelates, to be communicated by them to their respective seminaries, parishes, religious institutes, and priests; and that in their reports concerning the state of their respective dioceses or institutes, they should inform the Holy See concerning the execution of the matters therein determined."

Given at Rome, the 20th day of December, 1905.

Vincent
Card. Bishop of Palestrina, Prefect.
Cajetan De Lai,
Secretary

CHAPTER IV

THE OBLIGATION OF RECEIVING HOLY COMMUNION

ARTICLE 1. THE GENERAL OBLIGATION

An obligation may arise either from necessity as created by the very nature of man, or from precept as imposed by lawful authority. Man is obliged by necessity to take nourishment; he is obliged by precept to adore God. Both acts are necessary for the achievement of the purpose or end of his existence: he must eat to sustain his temporal life; he must adore God to gain eternal life. The common denominator of the two obligations lies in their quality of indispensability in the work of achieving a given end. The difference is found in the sources from which they immediately proceed.

This is not, of course, true of every precept emanating from whatsoever source; but when it is established that God is the author of a precept, as in the case given above, it takes on the characteristic of indispensability for the attaining of the end freely provided by God, as is the gift of eternal life.

Theologians have long disputed among themselves regarding the exact nature of man's obligation to receive the Sacrament of the Most Holy Eucharist. St. Thomas (1225-1274) carefully distinguished between the necessity of actually receiving the Sacrament and the wish or the desire to receive It. In theological terminology, man is bound by the necessity of means to the reception, not of the *sacramentum ipsum,* but of the *res sacramenti,* which, as St. Thomas explained, is the *unitas corporis mystici* to which all other sacraments are ordinated and outside of which there can be no salvation.[1]

This necessity is not the same as that which attaches to baptism, which is the door to the supernatural life, but it is a necessity which

[1]*Summa Theologica* (Diligenter emendata De Rubeis, Billuart et aliorum notis selectis ornata, 5 vols., Taurini: Ex officina libraria Marietti, 1933), Pars III, q. 73, art. 3.

arises through the reception of baptism and asserts itself following the attainment of the use of reason. For, as the Council of Trent declared, infants, regenerated by the waters of baptism and incorporated with Christ, cannot at that age (i.e. before attaining the use of reason) lose the grace acquired by them as sons of God.[2] On the other hand, adults cannot be excused from the obligation of communicating sacramentally if the occasion permits, for in the words of St. Thomas "a desire is in vain if it is not fulfilled when the opportunity is present."[3]

The *Roman Catechism* apparently endorsed this doctrine of St. Thomas when it stated, "We say that this Sacrament (of the Holy Eucharist) imparts grace, because even the *first* grace which all should have before they presume to approach this Sacrament, lest they 'eat and drink judgment to themselves,' is given to none unless they desire to receive the Holy Eucharist, which is the end of all the Sacraments, the symbol of ecclesiastical unity and brotherhood, to which anyone must belong if he is to attain divine grace."[4]

Vermeersch (1858-1936), while admitting that the more commonly current opinion of theologians[5] denies the inherent note of necessity in the nature of an essential means, even as explained by St. Thomas, and while content to vindicate the note of necessity which derives from precept alone in regard to the reception of the Holy Eucharist, nevertheless seems to favor the opinion of St. Thomas as being more in keeping with the words of Our Lord when He said, "Unless you eat the flesh of the Son of man and drink His blood, you shall not have life in you."[6]

[2]Sess. XXI, *de communione sub utraque specie et parvulorum*, c. 4.

[3]*Summa Theologica,* Pars III, q. 80, art. 11.

[4]*Catechismus Concilii Tridentini,* Lib. IV, *De Eucharistiae Sacramento*. nn. 51, 52.

[5]Cf. Capello, *Tractatus Canonico-Moralis de Sacramentis* (3 vols. in 6, Vol. I, 3. ed., Romae: Marietti, 1938), I, 421 (hereafter cited *De Eucharistia*).

[6]Vermeersch, *Theologiae Moralis Principia, Responsa, Consilia* (4 vols., Brugis: Charles Beyaert, 1927-1933; Vol. I, 3. ed., 1933; Vol. II, 2. ed., 1928; Vol. III, 2. ed., 1927; Vol. IV, 3. ed., 1933), III, 341-342 (hereafter cited *Theologia Moralis*).

Whatever the relative merits of the two opinions, the question is readily recognized to be of little more than academic importance. For it matters little whether one cannot attain eternal life without a true and effective desire to receive the Holy Eucharist, or whether he will not attain eternal life in consequence of his failure to obey a divine precept. In each case the result is the same.

Granted the serious obligation of receiving the Most Blessed Sacrament of the Eucharist, the question immediately arises, "When in a person's life does this obligation commence, and when is it acquitted? Does one Holy Communion satisfy the divine precept? And, if it does not, how frequently must one receive?"

Aside from the positive legislation of the Church, whose right and duty it is to determine specifically a general divine law, it is possible to derive from the divine precept itself, or, in following St. Thomas' reasoning, from the very nature of the sacrament, the obligation or the necessity of receiving the Holy Eucharist in two sets of circumstances. These two occasions, namely, when one is in danger of death and when one is beset with temptations to sin which cannot otherwise be overcome, are obviously relative factors in the individual's life and cannot form a basis for a numerical computation of the times when the obligation urges. They do, however, constitute a solid rule according to which the individual is able to judge his obligation to receive Holy Communion under pain of sin *hic et nunc,* that is, when these factors become operative in their demand.

In an attempt, therefore, to establish the minimum and maximum requirements of divine and ecclesiastical law regarding the frequency of receiving the Holy Eucharist, a more detailed, albeit brief, discussion of the above mentioned circumstances appears justifiable to the present writer. Having disposed of the less specific obligations, the discussion will turn immediately to a consideration of the specified requirements found in the Code of Canon Law.

A. *In Periculo Mortis*

While authors continue to hold varying opinions concerning the source of the obligation to receive Holy Viaticum when a person is in danger of death, not one of them suggests a denial of the obligation itself. Capello[7] and Coronata,[8] representing the more common opinion, declare that the obligation arises purely from divine precept. Vermeersch, on the other hand, indicating a preference for the theory of necessity in the nature of a means *saltem in voto,* stated that the nature of the obligation is more easily explained in the acknowledgment of the inherent necessity to fulfill the wish to receive Holy Communion if and when it becomes morally possible.[9] Augustine (1872-1943) departed from both views to hold that the obligation derives from a purely ecclesiastical precept.[10]

The common explanation of this obligation is clearly stated by Jorio, now Cardinal Prefect of the Sacred Congregation of the Sacraments, in his book concerning Holy Communion for the sick:[11] "Precisely how many times one must receive the Most Holy Eucharist in order to satisfy the divine precept, Jesus did not say. But it is beyond discussion that the moment in which the divine precept urges in all its force, is precisely when man girds himself for that great journey to eternity, that is, in the danger of death: for then is his eternal destiny at stake in the final war waged by the spirit of evil, who is determined in this last assault to make him his victim."

If this reasoning does not appear sufficient to establish a person's obligation of receiving Holy Viaticum in danger of death, the Code of Canon Law has removed all possibility of further

[7]*De Eucharistia,* pp. 422 ff.

[8]*Institutiones Iuris Canonici ad usum Utriusque Cleri et Scholarum De Sacramentis Tractatus Canonicus* (3 vols., Romae: Marietti, 1943-1946), I, 321 (hereafter cited *De Sacramentis*).

[9]*Theologiae Moralis,* II, 342.

[10]*A Commentary on the New Code of Canon Law,* (8 vols., Vol. IV, 2. ed., St. Louis: Herder Book Co., 1921), IV, 242 (hereafter cited *A Commentary on Canon Law*).

[11]*La Comunione agl' Infermi, Note Pratiche di Disciplina Sacramentale* (Romae: Pustet, 1931), p. 2. Translation from the Italian is present writer's own.

discussion by means of the positive enactment of canon 864, § 1:

> In danger of death, from whatever cause it may proceed, the faithful are bound by the precept of receiving Holy Communion.

Canonists and theologians alike use the terms "*in periculo mortis*" and "*in articulo mortis*" indiscriminately in relation to Holy Viaticum. For, in using the broader term, "*in periculo mortis*," the Code precludes any possible distinction in the matter. If one is bound "*in periculo mortis*," *a fortiori*, one is bound "*in articulo mortis*."

The phrase "*in periculo mortis*" is generally given a rather extensive interpretation. Cappello makes no attempt to compile an all-inclusive list of the circumstances which can constitute this danger of death, but he does mention as causes serious sickness, imminent battle,[12] childbirth (when it has been proved difficult from past experience, and generally when it is the mother's first parturition), surgical operations, death sentence, a raging pestilence, dangerous fire, hostile invasion, etc. He excludes, however, the average modern voyage by ship or airplane.[13]

At any rate, authors commonly agree that the danger of death spoken of in canon 864 cannot be restricted to a danger arising from only internal causes, but must include also all serious danger arising from any external cause. While this rule may seem to open the way for innumerable possibilities, it must not be pushed too far in practice. Vermeersch indicated that the danger must be true and imminent before it can be said that the obligation urgently calls for fulfillment. In speaking of the relaxation of the law of the Eucharistic fast for those who are in danger of death, he stated that "a true danger of death must be postulated as befalling them (i.e. when the danger arises *ab extrinseco*) to such a degree that

[12]A response of the Sacred Penitentiary, given on May 29, 1915, declared that every soldier who is in a state of warlike assembly or "mobilization" as it is called, can *ipso facto* be considered as in danger of death, so that he can be absolved by any priest he meets.—*Acta Apostolicae Sedis, Commentarium Officiale* (Romae, 1909-) VII, 282.

[13]*De Eucharistia*, pp. 422-423.

they can not conveniently expect to receive on the following day fasting."[14]

The obligation of receiving Holy Communion when one is in danger of death is certainly the minimum requirement that arises from the divine law. It will urge at least once in the life of every Catholic who has attained the use of reason, and perhaps several times in the lives of many.

B. *In Periculo Peccati*

The usefulness of the reception of Holy Communion as a means for avoiding future sins can scarcely be called into question. It is the nature of a sacrament to produce its effect *ex opere operato,* that is, through the very fact that a person has received it, and the solemn promise of Our Lord that "he who eats my flesh and drinks my blood has everlasting life"[15] could hardly be fulfilled except through a conquering of sin, which is, indeed, the spiritual death of the soul. As St. Thomas explained, the Eucharist, as a spiritual food, strengthens the spiritual life of man from within; and as the sign of Christ's passion and death, through which sin was conquered, It repels every attack of the devil.[16] It is, moreover, the teaching of many theologians that one of the effects of the act of receiving Holy Communion is the immediate and direct curbing and diminishing of the concupiscence of the flesh in the recipient.[17]

In view of these extraordinary graces inherent in the reception of Holy Communion, many authors, in company with St. Alphonsus,[18] assert that an obligation of communicating arises from the divine law as often as a person finds that Holy Communion is necessary for resisting some grave temptation to sin which he could not otherwise overcome.[19] This obligation, the authors admit, is

[14]*Theologia Moralis,* II, 336.

[15]St. John, VI: 55.

[16]Summa Theologica, Pars III, Q. 79, art. 6.

[17]Capello, *De Eucharistia,* 225.

[18]*Theologia Moralis* (5 vols., Augustae Taurinorum: Marietti, 1897), Lib. IV, n. 295.

[19]Capello, *De Eucharistia,* p. 423; Vermeersch, *Theologia Moralis,* II, 342-343.

purely incidental in character, but exists at the same time as an obligation which gathers its force from the strict obligation of the natural and positive divine law to avoid sin. Even so, the obligation could be said to urge only in so far as Holy Communion is found to be, in a particular case, a necessary remedy for overcoming the temptation to sin. Moreover, in theory at least, it is possible to supplant Holy Communion with other means for the overcoming of temptation, such as prayer and mortification. A third objection is to be found in the fact that a person who omits receiving Holy Communion, even though in his case it be absolutely necessary for the overcoming of temptation, could not be said to break the command to communicate, but only to sin against the virtue his particular weakness offended.[20] Cappello and Vermeersch, accordingly refrain from endorsing the opinion attributed to St. Alphonsus, and are content to urge frequent Communion as a most effective means of avoiding sin, without stating that under such circumstances Its reception is an obligation which derives from the divine law.

In view of the foregoing reasoning it becomes difficult to explain the common doctrine of theologians that even apart from the positive legislation of the Church the divine precept of receiving Holy Communion is of obligatory urgency several times (*pluries*) during a person's life.[21] The usual line of reasoning is that the divine precept calls for fulfillment several times during a person's life in as much as this Sacrament was instituted as a spiritual food and drink. It is clear from this, the authors say, that to take food and drink once is not sufficient, but one must receive several times in life in order to preserve, augment and restore his life. St. Thomas, however, objected to the use of this simile in view of the essential difference between material nourishment and the spiritual nourishment of Holy Communion. "Corporeal nourishment," he wrote, "is changed into the substance of the one nourished, and therefore it cannot contribute to the preservation of man's life unless he truly eats it. But spiritual nourishment

[20]Cappello, *De Eucharistia,* p. 424.

[21]Cappello, *ibid,* p. 422.

changes man into itself (*convertit hominem in seipsum*), according to the word of St. Augustine, who spoke as one hearing the voice of Christ telling him, 'You cannot change me into yourself, as you do food into your flesh, but you are changed into me.' But a man can be changed into Christ, and be incorporated in Him by a wish and desire of the will (*voto mentis*), even without the reception of this sacrament."[22]

Perhaps the point in question should not be over-stressed, for again it is of rather remote importance to the canonist. There is no written law to compel a person to use the Sacrament of the Holy Eucharist as a means toward overcoming temptation, even though it be a most salutary doctrine approved by the general practice of the Church. As for the obligation of receiving several times during life, the Church has deemed it expedient to enact positive legislation to enforce a practice which a not too well defined moral obligation once permitted to fall into a relatively expansive disuse.

C. The Paschal Precept

At a time in history when men were in grave danger of completely neglecting the reception of the Most Holy Eucharist throughout their entire lifetime,[23] the Church by exercising her divinely entrusted prerogative as pastor of souls and dispenser of the Sacraments obliged all of her subjects, under pain of severe penalties, to receive Holy Communion at least once a year. In reality this ecclesiastical precept specified for the first time for the universal Church the number of times that man is obliged to fulfill

[22]*Summa Theologica,* Pars III, q. 73, art. 3, *ad secundum.*

[23]Cf. *supra,* p 9; Pope Leo XIII called attention to this fact in his encyclical *Mirae caritatis,* issued on the 28th of May, 1902, when he wrote: "And indeed, it was a needful measure of precaution against a complete falling away that Innocent III, in the Council of the Lateran, most strictly enjoined that no Christian should abstain from receiving the Communion of the Lord's Body at least in the Paschal season."—*Fontes,* n. 648. (Hereafter, unless credit be given for the translation of a given passage, it may be presumed to be the present writer's own.)

the divine precept of communicating sacramentally.[24] Prior to the enactment of the IV General Council of the Lateran (1215) no obligation for the universal Church could be demonstrated.

Subsequent legislation has modified this first general enactment of the Church only to the extent of omitting the penal sanctions attached to it. The IV Lateran Council had enjoined the penalties of exclusion from the Church during life, and privation of Christian burial after death, upon those who were remiss in fulfilling their Easter duty. The Council of Trent[25] reaffirmed the enactment in its entirety, but the Code of Canon Law has omitted the penalties, thus rendering them unenforceable by reason of canon 6, 5°. Hence, it can no longer be taught or preached that a Catholic who omits his Easter duty for one year or for many is excommunicated and loses his right to Christian burial.[26]

The present obligation, as stated in canon 859, § 1, reads as follows:

> From the time that he attains the use of reason, each and every Catholic is bound to receive Holy Communion at least once a year at Easter, unless for some reasonable cause his pastor or confessor has advised him to abstain for a time.[27]

[24]*Conc. Lateranense* IV, can. 21: Omnis utriusque sexus fidelis, postquam ad annos discretionis pervenerit, omnia sua solus peccata saltem semel in anno fideliter confiteatur proprio sacerdoti, et injunctam sibi poenitentiam studeat pro viribus adimplere, suscipiens reverenter ad minus in Pascha Eucharistiae sacramentum, nisi forte de consilio proprii sacerdotis ob aliquam rationabilem causam ad tempus ab ejus perceptione duxerit abstinendum; alioquin et vivens ab ingressu ecclesiae arceatur et moriens christiana careat sepultura. Unde hoc salutare statutum frequenter in ecclesiis publicetur, ne quisquam ignorantiae caecitate velamen excusationis assumat . . . Mansi, XXII, 1007. This law was incorporated in the Decretals of Gregory IX as c. 12, X, *de poenitentiis et remissionibus,* V, 38.

[25]Sess. XIII, *de Eucharistia,* c. 9.

[26]Clinton, *The Paschal Precept,* The Catholic University of America Canon Law Studies, n. 73 (Washington, D.C.: The Catholic University of America, 1932), p. 39.

[27]Can. 859, § 1: Omnes utriusque sexus fidelis, postquam ad annos discretionis, idest ad rationis usum, pervenerit, debet semel in anno, saltem in Paschate, Eucharistiae sacramentum recipere, nisi forte de consilio proprii sacerdotis, ob aliquam rationabilem causam, ad tempus eius perceptione duxerit abstinendum.

While a complete commentary on the foregoing canon is not called for in this particular dissertation,[28] a few pertinent remarks may not be amiss. It will be seen from the canon quoted above that all who have reached the age of reason, even though they may not have completed their seventh year of age, are bound by this precept. The age of seven years supplies grounds for a presumption of the use of reason, but this presumption as invoked by the law must always yield to objective truth. More will be said in a later chapter regarding the amount of knowledge required in a child for the reception of Holy Communion.[29]

The precept is, moreover, double in character: it imposes an obligation of communicating at least once a year, and, secondly, states that this shall be done during the Paschal season. The importance of noting this fact is that, if a person is unable or unwilling to receive during the prescribed time, his obligation to receive later in the year does not cease. This is emphasized in paragraph 4 of canon 859: "The precept of Paschal Communion continues to bind, if any person did not fulfill it for any cause whatsoever during the prescribed time."[30]

Another point of significance is the faculty afforded the pastor or the confessor of quasi-dispensing a subject or penitent from the precept for a certain length of time. Vermeersch[31] remarked on this point that this power is not properly a faculty to dispense from the precept for any acceptable cause. Rather it is to be exercised by way of advice, and obviously for the spiritual advantage of the penitent. The words of the canon suppose that the postponement of fulfilling the precept is to be suggested by the pastor or the confessor, and not by the subject or the penitent who may

[28] A study of the Paschal Precept was made *ex professo* in 1932 by Clinton. Cf. preceding footnote, n. 26.

[29] *Infra*, p. 56.

[30] Can. 859, § 4. Praeceptum paschalis communionis adhuc urget, si quis illud praescripto tempore, quavis de causa, non impleverit.

[31] *Theologia Moralis*, II, 344.

find it inconvenient to make his Easter duty during the prescribed time.[32]

Article 2. For Persons in Special States of Life

From the foregoing article it will readily be seen that the general law of the Church makes no attempt to force upon the general laity the practice of frequent Holy Communion. A bare minimum is required, and this out of a profound desire to guide all to a fulfillment of the divine law. For those who have been called to a state in life requiring a higher degree of spiritual perfection, the Church has enacted a few special laws regarding a more frequent reception of Holy Communion. A cursory consideration of these laws seems fitting in this place.

A. Clerics

Fundamentally, the obligation of priests and other clerics to receive the Holy Eucharist more frequently than the laity is found, in law, in canon 124 of the Code of Canon Law. This canon imposes upon clerics the duty of leading a life interiorly and exteriorly more holy than that of laymen, and of excelling them in virtue and good example.[33] It is true that the obligation of receiving Communion, as implied in this canon, is only indirect and of an inferentially incidental character, but it cannot be denied that the excellency of this Sacrament and its inherent sanctifying power places frequent Holy Communion high on the list of necessary means for self-sanctification and good example.

Canon 805 imposes on priests the obligation of celebrating Mass several times a year, and further directs bishops and religious superiors to see to it that their subjects offer the Holy Sacrifice at least on Sundays and other feasts of precept.[34] This canon does

[32] Vermeersch-Creusen, *Epitome Iuris Canonici cum Commentariis ad Scholas et ad Usum Privatum*—(6. ed., 3 vols., Romae: H. Dessain, 1937-1946), II, 89 (hereafter cited *Epitome*).

[33] Can. 124. Clerici debent sanctiorem prae laicis vitam interiorem et exteriorem ducere eisque virtute et recte factis in exemplum excellere.

[34] Can. 805. Sacerdotes omnes obligatione tenentur Sacrum litandi pluries per annum; curet autem Episcopus vel Superior religiosus ut iidem saltem singulis diebus dominicis aliisque festis de praecepto divinis operentur.

not directly contemplate the priest's obligation of receiving Holy Communion, but it goes without saying that he who is obliged to celebrate Mass must also receive the Body and Blood of Christ.

The common interpretation of "several times a year" (*pluries per annum*) places the minimum requirement at three or four times a year.[35] The injunction that the bishop and the religious superior take care (*curet*) that their priests celebrate Mass on Sundays and other days of precept does not impose a strict obligation on the priests to say Mass on these days. The canon makes this clear by stating, first what is of obligation, and secondly what is the desire of the Church.

It is true, that by reason of canons 127 and 128 the bishop could oblige a priest to celebrate Mass on Sundays and days of precept if, in consequence of a scarcity of priests, it were necessary to provide Mass for the faithful.[36] Likewise it is evident that pastors and others who are bound by reason of their office to provide Mass for the faithful and to offer Mass for them on specified days are by indirect precept bound to receive the Holy Eucharist.[37] But aside from these or similar circumstances, the bishops and religious superiors would seem to exceed the legislator's intention as expressed in canon 805 if they were to use means more stringent than exhortations and mild admonitions to encourage their priests to a frequent celebration of Mass.

Two other canons in relation to the reception of Holy Communion on the part of clerics on particular occasions may here be considered. Canon 862 states that it is fitting (*expedit*) that all clerics, including those priests who do not celebrate Mass on that day, should receive Holy Communion on Holy Thursday at the

[35]Cappello, *De Eucharistia,* p. 620.

[36]Can. 127. Omnes clerici, praesertim vero presbyteri, speciali obligatione tenentur suo quisque Ordinario reverentiam et obedientiam exhibendi.

Can. 128. Quoties et quandiu id, iudicio proprii Ordinarii, exigat Ecclesiae necessitas, ac nisi legitimum impedimentum excuset, suscipiendum est clericis ac fideliter implendum munus quod ipsis fuerit ab Episcopo commissum.

[37]Cf. cann. 240; 339, § 1; 323, § 1; 306; 315; 440; 466, § 1; 471, § 4; 473, § 1.

solemn or conventual Mass. It should be noted here that the obligation imposed by the *Caeremoniale Episcoporum* upon the clergy of cathedral churches to receive Holy Communion at the solemn Mass on Holy Thursday is in no way abrogated by the absence of all mention of this obligation in canon 862.[38]

Bound by a strict obligation to receive Holy Communion on the occasion of their ordination Mass are all clerics promoted to major orders.[39]

B. Religious

The same general obligation as incumbent on clerics to lead a more perfect life than the laity is also incumbent upon all religious. This obligation is made clear in canons 592 and 593 of the Code. The chief means of achieving this more perfect life are, according to canon 593, fidelity to the religious vows and a life in accordance with the rules and constitutions of one's proper order or congregation. While religious superiors are obliged to promote frequent, and even daily, Communion among their subjects,[40] the Code has not only refrained from making frequent Communion mandatory, but has explicitly forbidden the old practice of assigning days on which all members of a community must, according to rule, receive Communion. According to the present legislation, if in the rules and constitutions of some religious orders or congregations there are found certain fixed days on which all must receive Holy Communion, such days are to be considered as designated merely directively and not in any way preceptively.[41]

While it is obviously the desire of the Church that religious receive the Holy Eucharist frequently, it has made no law requiring more of religious than is exacted of the ordinary laity. Since in this matter absolute freedom of conscience is of prime importance, the Chuch has consistently abstained from enacting legislation

[38] *Caeremoniale Episcoporum* (Romae: Pustet, 1886), II, c. XXIII, n. 6.

[39] Can. 1005. Omnes ad maiores ordines promoti obligatione tenentur sacrae communionis in ipsa ordinationis Missa recipiendae.

[40] Can. 595, § 2.

[41] Can. 595, § 4.

which might encroach upon a person's right to receive or to abstain from receiving Communion, according as he views the state of his soul at that moment. Indeed, the regulations of law enacted for the sake of protecting this freedom among religious—of which more will be said in a later article—are more plentiful and more exacting than those urging frequent Holy Communion.[42]

C. Seminarians

The Code of Canon Law imposes upon a bishop the duty of encouraging his seminarians to receive Holy Communion frequently.[43] The wording of the canon is similar to that of canon 805, according to which a bishop is to take care (*curet*) that his priest subjects celebrate Mass on Sundays and other holy days of obligation. Obviously, then, no strict obligation is intended to be placed upon the seminarians. It is rather the intention of the lawgiver through the ruling of canon 1367, 2°, to foster a practice of frequent Holy Communion among them. Aside from this one prescription, there is no law that requires of seminarians a reception of Holy Communion which is more frequent than that which the common law of the Church enacts as obligatory for all.

[42]Cf. *infra*, pp. 120 ff.

[43]Can. 1367, 2°.

CHAPTER V

THE LIMITATIONS OF CANON LAW ON THE RECEPTION OF HOLY COMMUNION

The memorable decree of Pope Pius X, *Sacra Tridentina Synodus,* constituted, in essence, an invitation to "all the faithful, of whatever rank and condition of life" to make use of frequent and daily Communion. It may be laboring the obvious to stress the fact that this general invitation is subject to the various limitations of law which the venerable Pontiff in no way intended to abrogate or minimize. For the decree makes no modifications in the pre-Code law regarding those persons who are prohibited from receiving Holy Communion, or in the circumstances under which it is prescribed that Holy Communion is not to be distributed. These laws remain in force. In some instances they have been even more sharply defined in the present Code of Canon Law.

The purpose of the following articles is to indicate briefly who, according to law, are incapable, unworthy or otherwise prohibited from receiving the Most Holy Eucharist; and, secondly, to mention those external circumstances which, in law, constitute a barrier to the reception of Holy Communion.

Article 1. Children and the Use of Reason

Canon 854, § 1, enacts a simple prohibition against the administering of the Holy Eucharist to children who because of their tender years do not yet possess an understanding of and relish for this Sacrament. In the two following paragraphs of the same canon, the Code defines the degree of understanding and relish which the child must possess in order licitly to receive Holy Communion. Paragraph 2 indicates the absolute minimum requirements, for it speaks of the most urgent circumstance conceivable, namely the danger of death. In this circumstance the child needs only to know how to distinguish the Eucharistic Body of Christ from ordinary food and how to adore It reverently. The third paragraph of canon 854 visualizes the child in the ordinary circumstances wherein the law requires a greater degree of knowledge and a more fitting preparation for Holy Communion. The canon requires that the child know, according to his mental capacity, those mysteries of faith which as means are necessary for salvation, and that he approach the Sacrament with a devotion in keeping with his youthful years.

It must be admitted that many practical difficulties arise from an honest attempt to apply these rules. The difficulty lies, not in an obscurity of the law, but in the power of recognizing the requisite qualities in the child. In a given case any doubt likely to arise is almost inevitably a doubt of fact and not a doubt of law. Hence it is that the obligation of solving such doubts must always be returned to those to whom the law explicitly entrusts it; namely, to the confessor, the parents and the pastor.[1]

Authors have long disputed regarding the signs which serve clearly to indicate a child's attainment of the use of reason. While the question is of great practical importance, the scope of the present work does not properly include a detailed discussion of it. It may be helpful, however, to note that the decree *Quam singulari* of August 8, 1910, which was directly concerned with Holy Communion for children, ruled that the obligation of the reception of the sacraments both of Communion (canon 859) and of Confession (canon 906) begin to oblige concomitantly when the child has gained the power of reasoning.[2] From this it can safely be deduced that, in judging whether the child has reached a sufficient maturity of mind to receive Holy Communion, the confessor may be guided by the child's capacity to commit sin. If this be evident, the requirement of a knowledge of the mysteries of faith can be easily supplied by means of adequate instruction.

[1]Can. 854, § 4-5.

[2]S.C. de Sacr., decr. 8 aug. 1910, n. I: "Aetas discretionis tum ad confessionem tum ad S. Communionem ea est, in qua puer incipit ratiocinari, hoc est circa septimum annum, sive supra, sive etiam infra. Ex hoc tempore incipit obligatio satisfaciendi utrique praecepto Confessionis et Communionis."—*Fontes*, n. 2103.

The age of seven years, it must be emphasized, merely constitutes grounds for a presumption of law that the child has attained the use of reason.[3] It is clear from the adherence of the pertinent canons to the phrases indicating the "use of reason" or the lack thereof,[4] and from the studied avoidance of specifying a definite age, that the legislators wished not to deprive any child, when it has attained the use of reason before reaching its seventh year, of its right to receive Holy Communion, and at the same time intended not to oblige anyone who, in spite of his seven years, had not yet reached the age of discretion.

According to canon 88, § 3, the totally insane are to be considered, in law, as infants, and as such are to be prohibited from the reception of Holy Communion. The *Roman Ritual* provides for those insane persons who have lucid intervals. If such persons have attained sufficient knowledge of the Sacrament, and externally manifest a devotion toward It, the *Ritual* permits the administration of the Holy Eucharist to them, provided that they actually be in a lucid interval and there be no danger of indignity to the Sacrament.[5]

A more complete discussion of the various problems encountered in dealing with the mentally incapacitated or retarded may be found in approved authors.[6]

Article 2. The Unworthy

Several classes of people are to be refused Holy Communion because of their unworthiness before the law. The Code of Canon Law, in canon 855, distinguishes between those who are publicly unworthy and those who are occult sinners. Canon 1956 empowers the local ordinary to prohibit persons guilty of certain grave delicts from the reception of Holy Communion according to the tenor of canon 2222, § 2. Finally, in canon 856 the prohibition which bars

[3]Can. 88, § 3.

[4]Can. 854, § 1: "*aetatis imbecillitatem*"; § 4: "*usum rationis*"; can. 859, § 1: "*Postquam ad annos discretionis*"; can. 906: "*postquam ad annos discretionis.*"

[5]Tit. IV, cap. 1, n. 10.

[6]Cf. Cappello, *De Eucharistia*, pp. 410-416.

anyone who is conscious of being in the state of mortal sin is stated. The first two mentioned canons concern the minister of Holy Communion and oblige him to refuse such persons the Most Blessed Sacrament. The last mentioned canon obviously concerns all possible subjects of Holy Communion, and must be applied by the individual to himself.

The "publicly unworthy" as mentioned in canon 855 are those who are excommunicated, who are under personal interdict, and who are manifestly branded with infamy, as long as it is not evident that they have repented and amended their ways and also previously counteracted and offset the earlier public scandal.[7] No distinction is made in this canon between those who have incurred the penalty of excommunication by way either of a *latae sententiae* or of a *ferendae sententiae* penalty, or against whom this penalty has or has not been authoritatively declared. Nor is any distinction made between the *"excommunicatus vitandus"* and the *"excommunicatus tolerandus,"* or between reserved and non-reserved censures. In all cases alike the excommunicate is to be refused if the fact of his unworthiness is publicly known as is apodictically stated in canon 2260.

In like manner persons under personal interdict are to be refused Holy Communion, according to canons 855 and 2275, § 2. Local interdict does not prohibit the reception of Holy Communion by those living in the interdicted place; nor does it forbid the administration of the Sacrament in the cathedral, in parish churches, or in a church which happens to be the only one in an interdicted town.[8]

Also to be refused Holy Communion are those persons who have incurred the penalty of infamy, whether in law or in fact. It matters not whether the penalty was automatically incurred in consequence of some violation to which the penalty attaches,

[7]Can. 855, § 1: Arcendi sunt ab Eucharistia publice indigni, quales sunt excommunicati, interdicti manifestoque infames, nisi de eorum poenitentia et emendatione constet et publico scandalo prius satisfecerint.

[8]Canon 2271, 2°

whether it was contracted in consequence of a condemnatory sentence, or whether it stands certified by means of an authoritative declaration made in or outside an ecclesiastical court. If there be manifest public knowledge that a person is branded with infamy, then such a person is barred from the reception of Holy Communion as long as a true and effective repentance has not preceded.[9]

It must be noted in relation to all the aforementioned categories of unworthy persons that the note of publicity or notoriety must accompany their disqualification before they can be publicly refused the Sacrament. According to the general norm enunciated by Pope Benedict XIV (1740-1758), a sinner is a public and notorious sinner (a) if he has been declared such by a competent ecclesiastical judge, or (b) if he has publicly confessed his crimes (i.e. made a judicial confession according to canon 1750), or (c) if he has committed in word or deed a crime that still exists in the knowledge of the public as not atoned for and therefore continues to be a source of scandal.[10] The conclusion to be drawn from the foregoing definitions is, then, that a reasonable number of the congregation, as well as the priest, must be aware of a person's unworthiness before the latter can be publicly refused the Sacrament.

Canon 855, § 2, directs priests to refuse the administration of the Sacrament to occult sinners[11] if they should petition Its reception privately; not, however, if they present themselves publicly for Its reception, for then the refusal to accede to their request would be accompanied with likely scandal.

Canon 856 forbids the reception of Holy Communion by anyone who is conscious of being in the state of mortal sin. It states,

[9]In can. 2343, § 1, 2° (who lay violent hands on the pope), in can. 2343, § 2, 2° (who similarly assault a cardinal or a legate of the Roman Pontiff), in can. 2351, § 2 (those who have engaged in duelling or acted as seconds), in can. 2356 (bigamists) and in can. 2357 (those who have been legitimately condemned for certain specifically qualified crimes in violation of the sixth Commandment). All the foregoing are branded with infamy in law. Cf. can. 2293, § 2. Can. 2293, § 3, points to those who are branded with infamy in fact.

[10]Ep. encycl. *omnibus,* 16 oct., 1756, § 4—*Fontes,* n. 441.

[11]According to can. 2197, 4°, all who are not public sinners.

further, that ordinarily sacramental absolution is required before one approaches the Holy Eucharist, even though one might be convinced that his act of perfect contrition and sorrow actually had restored the state of grace in his soul. The canon does, however, make it possible to forestall the further sin and possible scandal to which a too iron-clad enforcement of that principle could sometimes lead. If a real necessity for the receiving of Holy Communion[12] urges, and if at the same time there is no suitable confessor available,[13] a person may, without sin, receive Holy Communion after eliciting an act of perfect contrition.

The question of refusing Holy Communion to women and girls who present themselves in immodest attire belongs more properly to the field of moral theology. However, in so far as it

[12]Augustine stated that an urgent necessity of receiving Holy Communion exists when one has to fulfill the paschal obligation, and before contracting marriage,—*A Commentary on Canon Law,* IV, 233.

Cappello mentions the following circumstances as constituting an urgent necessity: (1) the danger of death for whatsoever cause and the impossibility of confessing or of receiving absolution; (2) scandal or infamy likely to arise from omitting the reception of Holy Communion; for example, a person already at the Communion rail remembers some mortal sin not yet forgiven; (3) a lack of time to go to confession joined with a real necessity of communicating.—*De Eucharistia,* p. 445.

Vermeersch remarked that the necessity of communicating would not occur as frequently as the necessity of celebrating Mass. Expressing a fear, moreover, that a too free invocation of "urgent necessity and a lack of opportunity for confession" might lead to grave abuse, he cited, as a safe principle to follow, the rule of Father Arregui as found in his *Summarium,* n. 545: "the necessity of communicating is considered present when one cannot omit Communion apart from arousing serious notice or grave suspicion (*sine gravi nota vel suspicione*)."—*Theologia Moralis,* III, 332, 333. Cf. Arregui, *Summarium Theologiae Moralis* (13. ed. reprint, Westminster, Md.: The Newman Bookshop, 1944), p. 360. ". . . communicandi [necessitas] . . . censetur haberi, cum sine gravi nota vel suspicione Communionem omittere non possis."

[13]The exemption owing to the absence of a suitable confessor (*copia confessarii illi desit*) certainly excludes the obligation of confessing to (1) a priest lacking jurisdiction; (2) a priest who is under a censure of excommunication as a *vitandus*; (3) an accomplice in *peccato turpi*; (4) a priest ignorant of the only language known to the penitent. The question of grave embarrassment due to close familiarity or similar circumstances is fully treated by the moral theologians. Cf. Vermeersch, *Theologia Moralis,* III, 266-269. Werts, "Insuperable Embarrassment and Confession," *Theological Studies,* IV (1943), 511-524; Dooley, "Priests in the Confessional," *The American Ecclesiastical Review* (*The Ecclesiastical Review,* from July, 1906-December, 1943) Philadelphia, 1884-1943; Washington, 1944- ; CIX (1943), 366-373.

indirectly applies here, the following may be stated. The Sacred Congregation of the Council, in an instruction given on January 12, 1930, issued a set of regulations intended to discourage the trend toward immodesty in women's dress. In these regulations number IX reads: "Girls and women who are immodestly dressed are to be refused Holy Communion and excluded from the office of sponsor in the sacraments of baptism and confirmation; and in proper cases are even to be excluded from the church."[14]

Article 3. The Eucharistic Fast

A. The General Law

Another important limitation placed on the recipient of Holy Communion is the required natural fast from midnight. Canon 858, § 1, states the general prohibition which prevents all non-fasting persons from receiving Holy Communion. This general prohibition makes no distinctions. Hence, the taking of any food, drink or medicine, which is orally administered, suffices to break this fast. The Eucharistic fast is broken when one has taken even a very slight amount of food, or drink, or of medicine.[15] It should be noted, however, that four conditions must be present before one breaks his fast: (1) the matter taken must be in the nature of food, drink or medicine; (2) the substance must be taken *ab extrinseco*; (3) it must be transmitted to the stomach; (4) it must be taken by way of an act of eating or drinking.[16]

The method of fixing midnight, or the time when the obligation of fasting commences, is indicated in canon 33, § 1: . . . *in sacra communione recipienda et in ieiunii vel abstinentiae lege servanda, licet alia sit usualis loci supputatio, potest quis sequi loci tempus aut locale sive verum sive medium, aut legale sive regionale sive aliud extraordinarium.* Hence, one who intends to communicate on the following day may eat or drink until the immediately preceding midnight figured according to any recog-

[14]Bouscaren, *The Canon Law Digest,* I, 213.

[15]Vermeersch-Creusen, *Epitome,* II, 84.

[16]Anglin, *The Eucharistic Fast,* The Catholic University of America Canon Law Studies, n. 124 (Washington, D.C.: The Catholic University of America Press, 1941), pp. 59-76.

nized manner of computing time. It is to be noted, however, that the hour of midnight is to be reckoned in accord with standards of physical accuracy, and not only according to the mere demands of a moral approximation.[17]

After stating the general prohibition, canon 858 admits of two exceptions from the Eucharistic fast. The first exception concerns the administration of Holy Viaticum to those in danger of death. A brief discussion of the circumstances constituting a danger of death has been presented earlier in this work.[18] It is sufficient to note here that whenever the obligation of receiving Holy Viaticum is established as urgent, the law of the Eucharistic fast ceases to apply.

The second exception to the law of the Eucharistic fast as contained in canon 858, § 1, provides for the exigency of consuming the Blessed Sacrament in order to safeguard it from irreverence. Anglin remarks that such a necessity would exist, for example, if a church were on fire or about to be destroyed by invading hordes or mobs, leaving no time to remove the Blessed Sacrament to a safe place. The law of fasting before Communion, which was made to insure a due reverence for the Holy Eucharist, ceases to bind when by its observance in such extraordinary cases the Blessed Sacrament could certainly be subjected to irreverence.[19]

Further exceptions to the law of the Eucharistic fast, relative to the priest and the celebration of Mass, are contained in the Rubrics of the *Roman Missal*. These exceptions pertain to: (1)

[17] Anglin, *The Eucharistic Fast,* p. 94.

[18] *Supra,* p. 46; cf. also Anglin, *The Eucharistic Fast,* pp. 95-104.

[19] Anglin, *The Eucharistic Fast,* p. 104. Mention should also be made of an exception from the Eucharistic fast as stated in the *Roman Ritual.* In the baptism of adults, the *Ritual* prescribes that a pinch of blessed salt be placed in the mouth of the catechumen. In accordance with the prescription of the *Ritual,* when the ceremony of baptism has been completed, Mass is to be celebrated if the hour proves suitable, and the newly baptized neophyte is to assist at the Mass and receive Holy Communion. The salt which is given to a newly baptized convert certainly does break the Eucharistic fast. However, when the Church made its liturgical laws, it tacitly in so far as it was necessary, dispensed from the law of the Eucharistic fast.—S.C. de Prop. Fide, *instr.* (ad Vic. ap. Tunkin, Orient.), 16 febr. 1806—Collect., n. 687.

the completion of the Holy Sacrifice of the Mass; (2) the case in which invalid matter is used for the Sacrifice; and (3) the consumption of the particles of the Sacred Host after the Communion of the Mass.[20]

B. Special Concessions for the Sick

Shortly after the issuance of the Decree *Sacra Tridentina Synodus*, there was raised the question of modifying the general law of fasting before Holy Communion in favor of the sick, so that they might be permitted to receive without the obligation of observing the Eucharistic fast in its entirety. In the resulting decree, *Post editum,* issued through the Sacred Congregation of the Council on December 7, 1906, Pope Pius X granted a concession whereby the sick who had been confined to bed for a month and whose state of sickness furnished no hope of a speedy recovery could be allowed to receive Holy Communion, though they had found it necessary to take some liquid food beforehand. The decree provided that they could under these circumstances receive once or twice a month if they were living in their homes, and once or twice a week if they lived in a religious house, a hospital or some other place in which the Blessed Sacrament was habitually reserved, or if they enjoyed the privilege of having Mass celebrated in a domestic oratory.[21]

A response of the Sacred Congregation of the Council later declared that the term "*decumbentes*" in the concession included not only those who were habitually confined to their beds, but also those who on account of the nature of their illness could not remain in bed, and those who were able to be up for a few hours each day, provided that the physician judged they could not keep the natural fast.[22]

The concession granted by Pope Pius X in 1906 is now contained in canon 858, § 2, of the Code of Canon Law: "The sick

[20]A complete treatment of these exceptions can be found in Anglin's treatise cited above.

[21]S.C.C decr. 7 dec. 1906—*Fontes,* n. 4331.

[22]S.C.C., 6 mart. 1907—*Acta Sanctae Sedis,* (41 vols., Romae, 1865-1908), XL (1907), 344.

who have been confined to bed for a month without the certain hope of a speedy recovery may, with the prudent advice of the confessor, receive Holy Communion once or twice a week though they have taken medicine, or some liquid food beforehand."

There are important changes in the law as granted by the Code. In the first place, there is no distinction made between the sick who are living at home and those who are in a religious house, a hospital, or some other place where the Blessed Sacrament is habitually reserved, or those who enjoy the privilege of having Mass celebrated in a domestic oratory. Hence, all the sick who qualify under the description in the Code may receive as often as twice a week without being subjected to the necessity of fasting. Likewise, the Code grants that medicine, whether liquid or solid, may be taken as well as liquid foods.

In summing up the classes of persons who qualify as *"infirmi"* in the sense in which this term is used in canon 858, § 2, Anglin states that the following may make use of the privilege: (1) Those who habitually are confined to bed by their illness, whether or not their illness be grave, and independently of the nature or origin of their sickness; (2) those who because of the peculiar nature of their sickness cannot remain in bed, e.g. asthmatics, provided that in the judgment of their physician their illness is grave; and (3) those who are seriously ill, but who are able to be up for a few hours each day.[23]

The question of whether a sick person must be unable to keep the natural fast before he can avail himself of the privilege of communicating without fasting is discussed at some length by Anglin.[24] While he notes that Cappello and Vermeersch hold that the privilege may be used by those who qualify under the wording of the canon even though they may be able to keep the fast, he feels that this interpretation is too extensive if it be applied to all categories of the sick. He argues that since the response of the

[23] *The Eucharistic Fast,* p. 127.

[24] *Ibid.,* pp. 139-140.

Sacred Congregation of the Council in 1907,[25] which interpreted the original concession of Pope Pius X to include "those who on account of the nature of their illness could not remain in bed, and those who were able to be up for a few hours a day," contained the explicit proviso that the physician judge that they could not keep the natural fast; and since the rules of interpretation in canon 6, 3°, order an adherence to the interpretation of earlier law when the later law agrees with it, in consequence only those sick persons who are habitually confined to bed have the privilege of receiving Communion without keeping the fast, even if they are able to fast without injury to their health.

Anglin's arguments are not without merit, but, in the present writer's opinion, are not conclusive enough to render the opinion of Vermeersch and Cappello untenable.[26] It may be noted, however, that if a confessor should find himself beset with an insoluble doubt in this matter, he can advise the person to apply for a dispensation which will be freely granted through the Apostolic Delegate.

Canon 858, § 2, explicitly states that this privilege should not be used without the advice of a prudent confessor. This is in keeping with the general practice of the Church, which, while eager to open the way to the reception of Holy Communion for all, always exercises great diligence lest abuses in relation to the Most Blessed Sacrament arise through ignorance or misguided zeal.

A private response of the Pontifical Commission for the Interpretation of the Code ruled that a moral rather than a mathematical computation of the term "*a mense*" was permissible in this canon.[27] Anglin furnishes a very thorough and satisfactory treatment of this problem in his work already cited, and concludes that it is sufficient if a person has been sick for twenty-six or twenty-seven days in order to avail himself of the privilege granted in canon 858, § 2. He also concludes that a moral continuity of the month's

[25]*Supra*, p. 64, *in fine*.

[27]P.C.I., 24 nov. 1927—Bouscaren, *The Canon Law Digest*, II, 215.

[26]Cf. Vermeersch, *Theologia Moralis*, III, 339; Cappello, *De Eucharistia*, pp. 470-474.

illness is sufficient to allow a use of the indult. Thus, if a person were confined to bed for many days of the month, but during that time enjoyed a few days of better health, he could in all probability use the privilege under discussion.

Two recent decrees of the Sacred Congregation of the Sacraments have extended the exemption from the Eucharistic fast to include two classes of people hitherto not eligible under canon 858, § 2.

The first decree, granted by His Holiness, Pope Pius XII, in an audience on March 25, 1946, and issued through the Most Reverend Apostolic Delegate on May 17, 1946, extended, for a period of three years, to the Most Reverend Ordinaries of the United States, the faculty to grant dispensations from the Eucharistic fast, to the extent of taking liquid foods and medicine,[28] to those persons who are hospitalized for reasons of health, and provided that any occasion of grave scandal or wonderment on the part of the faithful be removed.[29]

This grant, it will be noted, is given by way of a faculty to the Most Reverend Ordinaries, and not directly as a privilege to all the faithful who are being hospitalized for reasons of health. Hence, no one may invoke it directly for himself, nor can a priest

[28]Commenting in the *Revue Eucharistique du Clergé* (XLIX [1946], 433) on a similar indult granted to the Ordinaries of Canada and Newfoundland, Moise Roy, S.S.S., furnishes an authoritative interpretation of the term "liquid foods": "The dispensation as accorded permits the sick to receive Communion after having taken beverages or medicines (even when the latter contain alcohol), but not after taking solid nourishment (except when this would be a medicament). By *beverage,* drink or liquid, one may understand, according to a declaration made by the Holy Office on September 7, 1897, [*Fontes,* n. 1192] water, wine, milk, tea, coffee, other brews, fruit or vegetable juices, the various bouillons (excluding meat bouillons on days of abstinence, except when there is another dispensation), syrups and even liquids which contain a solid substance in suspension, such as bread crumbs (grated bread) or chocolate, or also whipped eggs, cream of wheat and thin gruels, provided that all this maintains the consistency of a liquid and can be drunk from a glass."

[29]*The Jurist,* VI (1946), 423. By an extension of this privilege the Most Reverend Ordinaries can now dispense for the reception of Holy Communion [not for the celebration of Mass], according to the terms of the faculty, priests confined by illness to their rectory or to a religious or private house.—Letter from Apostolic Delegation, April 3, 1947.

invoke it in favor of a second party without having first received the proper delegation of this faculty from his lawful ordinary.[30]

According to the general norms of interpretation found in the first book of the Code of Canon Law, habitual faculties, such as the one under consideration, are to be considered privileges *praeter ius*[31] and should in any case of substantial doubt regarding their meaning and application receive a liberal interpretation in accord with the norm of Canon 68. Hence the grant of power contained in the new faculty may be given a liberal interpretation. The individual dispensations, however, which the ordinaries may grant through their use of this faculty must receive a strict interpretation in accordance with canon 85.

The method of granting dispensations in this matter is not specified in the letter of the Apostolic Delegate, so it may be assumed that the ordinaries may proceed according to their own discretion under the law. A subdelegation of this power to dispense is permissible by reason of canon 199, § 2,[32] and appears desirable in a matter of this kind. Indeed, should need or advantage to the Church indicate the helpfulness of a very wide subdelegation of this faculty, it would be difficult to demonstrate why an ordinary could not subdelegate all of his priest subjects for the entire three year period.

[30]This faculty, without the condition of hospitalization, was enjoyed by all military chaplains by reason of their special war-time faculties: "Concedendi infirmis ut Ss.mam Eucharistiam quotidie recipere possint, etiamsi aliquam medicinam vel aliquid per modum potus antea sumpserint."—*Facultates Castrenses* (editio altera, commentario aucta, New York, 1942) Part II, p. 14, n. 16.

Chaplains of the Navy have, by reason of their ordinary military faculties, the power "to dispense from the Eucharistic Fast, in individual cases, and in accordance with your own prudent judgment, whenever the weather is oppressive, avoiding all danger of scandal and wonderment, those belonging to the naval services stationed in the Philippine Islands, who must rise early in the morning to perform their laborious naval duties, so that they can take some liquids on Sundays and Holy Days of Obligation before the reception of Holy Communion."—*Facultates Castrenses*, Part I, p. 5, n. 11.

[31]Can. 66, § 1.

[32]Can. 199, § 2: Etiam potestas iurisdictionis ab Apostolica Sede delegata subdelegari potest sive per actum, sive etiam habitualiter, nisi electa fuerit industria personae aut subdelegatio prohibita.

The present writer, however, is inclined to feel that such an indiscriminate use of the faculty to dispense would offend against the spirit of the general law of the Eucharistic Fast and the faculty itself. The Eucharistic Fast has long been popularly regarded as a strict law, and the Holy See until recent years had reserved to itself the power of dispensing from it. Any departure from such a strict discipline seems to demand a gradual and judicious treatment, lest it become a source of abuse. As will be seen presently, the conditions under which ordinaries may grant dispensations from the fast are open to a variety of interpretations and, as such, might be subject to imprudent extension or restriction if the faculty were too freely shared with others. It may be argued further that, since the commonly accepted practice regarding the issuing of dispensations through the faculties as contained in the grant of the Quinquennial Faculties to ordinaries limits the use of these faculties to the ordinary and a few qualified delegates, it would be difficult to see why a wholesale subdelegation of this triennial faculty should be made. The very fact that there was granted the faculty of dispensing rather than a general privilege seems to support the view that a discriminating and careful approach be made in this matter.

The new faculty makes it possible for a sick person, regardless of the length of time he has been ill or confined to bed, but provided that he now be in a hospital, to obtain a personal dispensation from the Eucharistic fast directly from the ordinary of the place or his lawful delegate. Hence, a person who has been suddenly stricken with illness and is immediately taken to a hospital, may be personally dispensed from the fast as soon as the occasion for receiving Holy Communion arises. Previously he would have had to be confined in bed for a month before enjoying the privilege bestowed in canon 858, § 2, as has been explained above, or he would have had to apply for a dispensation from the Apostolic Delegate. Once the sick person has received a dispensation under the new faculty, no limit other than that which is set by the common law needs to be respected regarding the number of times he may receive Holy Communion during the week.

There are, however, two important conditions specified in the grant of this privilege to dispense from the Eucharistic fast. First, the confinement in the hospital must be for reasons of health. This would preclude the dispensing of nurses, doctors and other persons who live in the hospital for reasons of work. It is clear, too, from the words "*pro infirmis . . . durante tantum male affecta valetudine*," that the person, in order to be validly dispensed, must be in a state of bad health. Ordinarily the question should not prove difficult to solve, since there are few who care to stand the expense of hospitalization—or who would even be admitted—without serious reason. There are, however, several classes of persons in hospitals about whom reasonable questions may arise. It would constitute an impossible task to compile an all-inclusive list of those who may and who may not be dispensed under the new faculty. However, a brief discussion of several cases may prove helpful in demonstrating the general principle involved, namely, that those who are sick and in a hospital may be dispensed during the time that they are afflicted with bad health.

Perhaps the most common case of a person being confined in a hospital for conditions other than pathological is that of expectant mothers. In a normal case of pregnancy and parturition, sickness, in the sense of ill health, does not exist. Any accompanying pain, weakness, or other symptoms commonly ascribed to ill health are in this case purely natural. Hence in all strictness one can argue that unless some pathological complication accompanies the pregnancy and birth, the mother could not be dispensed from the Eucharistic fast under the new faculty.

This, however, is a strict interpretation which seems not to fit well in relation to a privilege, as has been stated above.[33] Canon Mahoney, in reply to the question whether a priest may take Holy Communion to an expectant mother shortly before the child is expected, if she finds it difficult or inconvenient to come to the church, wrote: "Holy Communion may be taken to expectant mothers as to any other person in a condition of sickness or infirmity . . . In view of all we do, or ought to do, to encourage motherhood, it is obviously desirable to communicate expectant mothers

[33] P. 68.

who are unable to come to the church. Indults,[34] moreover, are easily obtainable permitting expectant mothers to communicate non-fasting in accordance with the conditions of canon 858, § 2, a practice which supports the view that they are equivalent to sick persons."[35]

Surely the arguments presented by Canon Mahoney apply in relation to the new indult. For if it has been the practice of the Holy See and of the Apostolic Delegate freely to grant expectant mothers the privilege of communicating non-fasting according to the tenor of canon 858, § 2, on the grounds that their condition is equivalent to that of sick persons, it would seem unreasonable to exclude them from eligibility under the new faculty in consequence of a narrower interpretation of the class of persons who are to be considered sick. Hence, it is the present writer's opinion that as long as the mother is confined in the hospital, before or after the birth of her child, she may be considered as a sick person and be dispensed from the Eucharistic fast according to the faculty under consideration.

It may be helpful to note here that the question of whether any patient in a hospital is actually able to keep the fast without grave inconvenience cannot be raised as a point at variance with this broad interpretation of the privilege.[36] The letter of the Apostolic Delegate makes no such distinction, and an interpretation which would make it seems to run contrary to canon 67, which forbids the restriction of a privilege as well as its extension. Hence a person suffering from broken bones or similar conditions, which do not long affect his ability to keep the fast, should not be refused a dispensation on that account. Neither should such persons be regarded as in a state of sound health simply because their infirmity is localized and does not produce a general condition of sickness. As long as they are confined to the hospital because of their infir-

[34]". . . in individual cases a dispensation may be obtained upon request for persons sixty or more years old, for pregnant and nursing mothers . . ."—Diekamp, *Katholische Dogmatik,* (3 vols., 7. and 8. eds., Munster, Aschendorff, 1934-1937), III, 169.

[35]Mahoney, "*Questions and Answers*"—*The Clergy Review,* XXII (1942), 560-561.

[36]Cf. *supra,* pp. 65-66.

mity, whatever be its nature, they may qualify under the broad terms of the privilege and become lawfully dispensed.

A somewhat similar case is that of convalescents, or of those who have passed well beyond the crisis of their illness and are confined to hospitals only to expedite their complete recovery. At first sight, the clause *"durante tantum male affecta valetudine"* may seem to imply an intentional exclusion of such patients from the use of the privilege. Canon 86, however, indicates that a dispensation which implies the successive repetition of a privileged act ceases—aside from the other methods in which privileges cease—only with the *certain* and *total* cessation of the motivating cause.[37]

In the privilege in question the motivating cause is unquestionably sickness qualified by the fact of hospitalization. Since convalescence is factually distinguishable from the state of sound health, and connotes in reality the last stage of an illness, it follows that, as long as the convalescent person remains in a hospital, the motivating cause cannot be said to have certainly and totally ceased. The clause *"durante tantum male affecta valetudine"* must be interpreted to exclude only those who remain in the hospital after they have certainly and completely reached a state of good health.[38]

[37]Can. 86. Dispensatio quae tractum habet successivum, cessat iisdem modis quibus privilegium, nec non certa ac totali cessatione causae motivae.

[38]The indult granted to the Ordinaries of Canada and Newfoundland is essentially the same as the indult granted to the Ordinaries of the United States. It reads as follows:

Ottavae, die 30 Julii 1946

Delegatio Apostolica
N. 1548/46

Excmis Ordinariis Ditionis Canadensis et Terrae Novae.

Sacra Congregatio de Sacramentis, per Ven. Rescriptum sub N. 2069/46 *die 4 Aprilis huius anni datum, infrascripto Delegato Apostolico commisit officium haec quae sequuntur communicandi*:

"SSmus Dominus Noster PIUS, Div. Prov. PP. XII, dignatus est concedere. ad triennium, *omnibus Ordinariis Ditionis Canadensis et Terrae Novae, facultatem dispensandi a lege ieiunii eucharistici* infirmos *in eorundem Dioecesium* nosocomiis *vel* valetudinariis degentes, ita ut *aliquid sumere ipsi possint, ante SS. Communionem,* per modum potus *vel* medicinae, durante male affecta valetudine, *remota quavis scandali vel admirationis occasione, servatisque ceteris omnibus de iure servandis."*

(*subscr.*) *Ildebrandus*
(*L.S.*) *D.A.*

Moise Roy, S.S.S., in commenting on this Canadian faculty, wrote as follows:

"A dispensation must not be given from an ecclesiastical law without a just and reasonable cause (c. 84). However, a medical prescription which must be observed or a real inconvenience in the keeping of the Eucharistic fast up until the moment of Communion always constitutes a sufficient cause for the granting of a dispensation. In case of doubt one may apply the presumption in favor of the hospitalized sick person. It is necessary also, as the rescript indicates, to avoid in the granting of this favor anything which might provoke wonderment or scandal among the faithful, and to observe to the letter all that is otherwise prescribed by the law, so that this heavenly nourishment shall not be received as ordinary bread, but rather with dignity and respect. It may happen, therefore, that one could sometimes dispense in a general fashion, and without any other particular disposition, all the sick who enter a hospital, or all those who occupy this or that department; however, as a general rule, it seems called for that one verify the circumstances, personally or through others, of all cases, and it is a matter of due moment not to apply the dispensation until one has become assured that the sick have need of it. One may, however, depend upon the proffered judgment of the nurse in this matter.

"This dispensation should not be accorded for too long a period at any one time, in order that one be in a position to verify, on occasion, the continued existence of the cause. A dispensation legitimately granted will nevertheless be valid for a particular case as long as the final or motive cause exists, even if the power of the one who granted the dispensation should in the meanwhile have expired (can. 86, col. can. 73)."—*Revue Eucharistique du Clergé,* XLIX (1946), 434-435.

It seems to the present writer that Father Roy, in the foregoing commentary, exacts a cause on the grounds of canon 84 which amounts to a restriction of the indult. For in granting the indult to dispense from the Eucharistic fast the Holy See itself must act in accord with canon 84. In declaring that only those sick persons who are hospitalized may be dispensed, the Holy See has established the just and reasonable cause, namely sickness and hospitalization. To exact over and above these conditions the need of taking medicine or the sustaining of a grave inconvenience in fasting seems unwarrantably to restrict the use of the indult. Reilly in his dissertation, *The General Norms of Dispensation* (The Catholic University of American Canon Law Studies, n. 119, Washington, D.C.: The Catholic University of America Press, 1939) remarks: "In general, the causes which are advanced for dispensations are either final (motivating) causes or accessory causes. The former are those which of themselves are sufficient to convince the superior that a dispensation is justified . . . (ibid., p. 106).

"In order that reasons for dispensations might measure up to the requirements of proportionate justice and reasonableness, it is not necessary that they be such as are sufficient to *excuse* one from the observance of a law . . . Nor need the reason be so weighty that the superior is, by relative necessity, obliged to grant the dispensation . . . In other words, the requirements of the cause are fulfilled if in view of the particular circumstances the observance of the law would (1) constitute a proportionately grave difficulty beyond the inconvenience commonly experienced in abiding by a law, or (2) impede some reasonably proportionate benefit which would result from the relaxation of the law." (ibid., pp. 107-108).

In view of the very nature of a privilege and the broad terms in which this particular one is stated, it seems that as few restrictions as possible should be made. Only those people who remain in a hospital as guests, or employees, or who come in good health for physical examination, precautionary x-rays and the like, or for mere rest and solitude, should be refused dispensations from the Eucharistic fast under the new faculty.

The second essential condition specified in the grant of the privilege to dispense in the manner under consideration is that the infirm person be actually in a hospital. Since there are various kinds of hospitals for the care of diversely afflicted persons, and since these hospitals are usually called by specific and sometimes euphemistic names, some speculation may easily arise regarding the exact extension of the word "hospital" (*nosocomium*) as used in the letter of the Apostolic Delegate.

Following the general rules of interpretation as stated in canon 49,[39] the proper meaning of *nosocomium,* as given in two complete and critical dictionaries, is a place in which the sick are received and cared for.[40] This broad definition of *nosocomium* is, etymologically at least, more inclusive than its nearest English equivalent, "hospital." Webster's *International Dictionary* and James A. H. Murray's *New English Dictionary on Historical Principles*[41] limit the extension of the word "hospital" to institutions, places or establishments for the care of the sick or wounded, or of those who

[39]Can. 49. Rescripta intelligenda sunt secundum propriam verborum significationem et communem loquendi usum, nec debent ad casus alios praeter expressos extendi.

[40]". . . locus in quo recipiuntur, curanturque pauperes aegroti, valetudinarium: a *nosos* morbus et *coméo* curo."—*Lexicon Totius Latinitatis,* (Aegidii Forcellini Seminarii Patavini Alumni cura et studio Lucubratum; deinde Josephi Furlanetto opera auctum et emendatum; tandem Francisco Corradini (Toms. I, II, III) et Josepho Perin (Tom. IV) ejusdem seminarii alumnis curantibus auctius emendatus melioremque in formam redactam, 19 vols., Patavii: Typis Seminariis, 1920), III-1, 390.

Nosocomion, Locus in quo aegroti curantur, Valetudinarium.—*Thesaurus Graecae Linguae* (ab H. Sephano constructus, 7 vols., editio nova auctior et emendatior, London: Valpianis, 1822), IV, col. 6422.

[41]2. ed., unabridged, Springfield, Mass.: Merriam Co., 1944; Oxford: The Clarendon Press, 1901.

require or are given medical or surgical care. A use of such a definition would necessarily lead to the establishment of a criterion based on the institution's therapeutic methods. It would exclude sanatoriums where rest and climate are the chief factors in the rebuilding of a patient's health. Asylums for the mentally afflicted might be excluded, as might an institution specializing in chiropractic treatments, or in the application of methods abstracting from the use of medicine or surgery. Such restrictions are not indicated in the grant of the faculty. They certainly seem out of keeping with the tenor of canon 67.

A broader view of the word *nosocomium,* as indicated in the privilege's use of *infirmi* (weak, infirm) as opposed to *aegroti* (sick, ill) would afford a less perplexing principle and one which at the same time does not imply any unjustifiable extension of the wording contained in the indult. Hence, it is the present writer's opinion that any institution or place specifically set aside for the habitual care of the infirm, as qualified in the preceding pages, may be considered a *nosocomium,* as contemplated in the faculty under discussion. All types of hospitals, therefore, whether they exist for the care of the physically sick, of the mentally incapacitated, of expectant mothers, or merely of convalescent patients, should suffice to fulfill the faculty's requirement of hospitalization. Infirmaries, too, provided that they be habitually set aside for the care of the sick, seem to qualify under the broad wording of the faculty.[42]

[42]In the first grant of this privilege to the Most Reverend Ordinaries of Canada and Newfoundland, given September 28, 1943, the subjects of the dispensations were described as "*fideles infirmi in nosocomiis eiusdem Ditionis degentes.*"

Commenting on this particular grant, Father Roy remarked in the *Revue Eucharistique du Clergé* (XLVII [1944] 93, footnote 1): "This dispensation cannot be accorded in hospices as such, but may be accorded in convalescent homes or hospitals. There is no longer any doubt that the large organized infirmaries in certain religious congregations for receiving all their sick members should be considered as true hospitals. But may one include in this privilege the smaller infirmaries which are established in conformity with the constitutions of the various religious houses? Since a hospital, "*nosocomium,*" is nothing more, according to the Greek etymology, than a place destined for the care of the sick (*nosocomeion*: infirmary), and since furthermore a power of dispensing, where it is not restricted to a determined case, may be interpreted in the wider sense (can. 85 and 66, § 1), it seems that this dispensation may be accorded to the sick in most of these religious infirmaries if they are confined and if they experience a serious difficulty in communicating while fasting."

The second grant of the same indult reworded the description of the subject as follows: ". . . infirmos *in eorundem Diocesium* nosocomiis *vel* valetudinariis degentes . . ." The word "*valetudinariis*" is not contained in the indult granted to the Ordinaries of the United States, but since this word is connected with the more generic term "*nosocomiis*" by means of the copulative "*vel*" it seems to serve more in the nature of an interpretation of the original than as an extension of its meaning. At any rate, it does not seem that one should exclude such places as are better described by the word "*valetudinariis*" simply because this word is not included explicitly in the indult.

Father Roy offers the following commentary on the meaning of these two words in the *Revue Eucharistique du Clergé* (XLIX [1946] 433): "According to this rescript, the Canadian Ordinaries have for a period of three years, as His Excellency, the Most Reverend Joseph Charbonneau, has indicated in the *Semaine Religieuse de Montreal* of September 25, 1946, 'the power of according (when they need it) the permission of receiving Communion even daily after having taken liquids or medicine, to sick persons confined to hospitals, clinics, infirmaries, and convalescent hospitals during their sickness.'

"This dispensation is valid for the sick '*in nosocomiis* vel *valetudinariis*.' These two words, etymologically, embrace all places which are destined for the care of the sick. This is to say, not only clinics and hospitals properly so called (with their annexes), but also the convalescent homes and infirmaries of religious communities (with their dependencies). As for foundling homes and hospices, although as such they do not enter into this category, there is reason nevertheless for sometimes including them at least partially when they do not serve merely for the boarding of infants and aged persons, but are in fact engaged in the care of the sick and helpless."

Regarding the various types of institutions commonly called "homes" or "asylums," their inclusion under the faculty seems hardly justifiable, unless the name were clearly an euphemism to cover the true nature of the institution's purpose. Thus homes for the aged, for the blind or for the deaf, could scarcely be accepted as places for the therapeutic care of the infirm. They are rather refuges for people who are too handicapped to make their way in the world. Needless to say, infirmaries in institutions of this kind would, as stated above, qualify as *nosocomia* in the broad sense. On the other hand, an asylum for lepers would qualify in itself by reason of the hopeful efforts habitually made to effect a cure.[43]

[43] A letter from the Apostolic Delegation under date of April 3, 1947, extended to the Most Reverend Ordinaries the power to dispense for the reception of Holy Communion, according to the terms of this faculty, priests confined by illness to their rectory or to a religious or private house.

A third condition stated in the letter of the Apostolic Delegate is that any occasion of grave scandal or wonderment of the faithful be removed. In a matter of this kind a removal of the occasion of scandal or wonderment could probably be most easily effected by means of a proper instruction of the nurses, doctors and patients involved. There is nothing to conceal. Indeed, an explanation of the Church's deep consideration for the sick and its desire for a more widespread use of frequent Communion should prove to be more edifying than bewildering. It is evident, however, that an uninformed doctor or nurse could readily be scandalized or at least suffer bewilderment in seeing a patient receive Holy Communion when they knew him not to be fasting. This is undoubtedly the situation against which the Delegate's letter warned, and one which could easily be forestalled by a bit of prudent instruction on the part of the hospital chaplain and the nursing sisters.

C. Indult Affecting Eucharistic Fast of Night Workers

On request of the Most Reverend Ordinaries of the United States, His Holiness, Pope Pius XII, granted, through the Sacred Congregation of the Sacraments, for a period of three years beginning July 26, 1946,[44] the faculty of dispensing from the natural fast those of the faithful who habitually work after midnight, in such a manner that they, abstaining from solid food for four hours previous to communicating, and from liquid for one hour, exclusive of all alcoholic beverages after midnight, may receive Holy Communion out of devotion on Sundays and other days of obligation and one other day of the week, the usual precautions against scandal and wonderment on the part of the faithful being taken.[45]

The following conditions for the exercise of this faculty to dispense were specified in the Apostolic Delegate's letter to the

[44]Date of execution by the Most Reverend Apostolic Delegate.

[45]"Metropolitae, Episcopi necnon alii Ordinarii locorum Foederatorum Americae Septentrionalis Statum, humiliter postulant benignam facultatem dispensandi a naturali ieiunio fideles habitualiter post mediam noctem laborantes, ut ipsi, abstinendo a cibis solidis per quatuor horas, et a potu per unam horam, et dummodo potus post mediam noctem sumptus nonalcoholicus sit, SS.am Communionem Eucharisticam recipere valeant ex devotione, remoto quocumque scandalo et admiratione."—*The Jurist,* VI (1946), 539.

Ordinaries, under date of July 26, 1946:

1. The Most Reverend Ordinaries, in granting dispensations under this faculty, must proceed in a way that is certain and determinate, not leaving the use of this privilege to the judgment of the faithful;
2. The dispensation may be given for Sundays and Feasts of Precept and for one other day during the week as the devotion of the individual communicant may dictate; furthermore, in the case of nursing Sisters dispensation may be granted for *daily* Communion whenever the previous night has been spent in service of the sick;
3. At the expiration of the faculty, a report is to be made to the said Sacred Congregation on the use of the faculty and on its advantages and possible disadvantages.[46]

Under this indult, the bishops and all other local ordinaries in the United States may issue dispensations from the Eucharistic fast, to the extent described above,[47] to any person (under their juris-

[46]*The Jurist, loc. cit.*

[47]The Most Reverend Ordinaries of Canada and Newfoundland enjoy a similar indult, granted on July 30, 1946. It contains several limitations not found in the indult to the Ordinaries of the United States, but in some other respects seems to be more liberal. Its substance, as reproduced in the *Revue Eucharistique du Clergé,* XLIX (1946), 435, is as follows:

"*SSmus Domnius Noster PIUS, Div. Prov. PP. XII, dignatus est concedere,* ad triennium, *omnibus Ordinariis Ditionis Canadensis et Terrae Novae, facultatem dispensandi a jejunio eucharistico* infirmorum ministros utriusque sexus—*praesertim sorores—qui* nocturno tempore *suo munere funguntur in eorundem Diocesium* nosocomiis *vel* valetudinariis, *ita ut ipsi SS. Communionem recipere possint etsi antea solidum* cibum *vel* potum, non alcoolicum, *sumpserint; servato tamen jejunio* quattuor horarum post cibi solidi sumptionem *et* unius saltem horae post sumptionem potus, non alcoolici.

"*Hisce conditionibus—ceterisque animae et corporis dispositionibus servatis—SS. Eucharistica Communio memoratis infirmorum ministris permitti poterit* diebus dominicis *et* festis de praecepto, *vel* alia die in hebdomada, *juxta Christifidelium devotionem. Si vero agatur de Sororibus religiosis, SS. Communio permitti poterit, juxta memoratas conditiones, etiam* singulis diebus *successivis ea undem nocturno servitio continuo.*"

The first difference from the indult accorded to the Ordinaries in the United States to be noted is the subjects to whom the dispensation may be granted. The indult to the United States requires only that the subjects be habitually engaged in work after midnight, regardless of the type of work. The Canadian indult may be applied only to "*ministri infirmorum.*" Father Roy, basing his commentary in the *Revue Eucharistique du Clergé* (XLIX [1946], 436-437) on the interpretation offered by Archbishop Charbonneau, wrote as follows: "By '*ministri infirmorum*' may be understood intern physicians, orderlies of either sex, professional nurses, either graduate or student, and also—so it seems—all persons whose presence is necessary during the night for the normal functioning of the hospital service of the institution." He adds in a footnote: "This excludes men employed in maintenance (la refection des

diction)[48] who habitually works after midnight and is not otherwise excluded by law. By virtue of canon 199, § 2, this faculty may be subdelegated to priests of the ordinary's jurisdiction, but only in such a way that an accurate account of the dispensations can be preserved, since a report of its use must be made to the Sacred Congregation of the Sacraments at the end of the three year period for which the faculty is granted.[49]

immeubles) and persons charged with the general cleanliness of the house, but may include, to our mind, the telephone operator, the hospital attendant in charge of admitting the sick and even the boiler attendants (less chauffeurs de fournaises)."

Another important difference in the two indults lies in the use of "*nocturno tempore suo munere funguntur*" in the Canadian indult, and "*habitualiter post mediam noctem laborantes*" in the indult accorded to the United States. Father Roy comments: "Night service should generally be understood as work done after the hour of midnight, that is to say, terminated after this hour or begun at midnight . . . But the new indult . . . speaks only of work done '*nocturno tempore.*' It seems therefore that one may sometimes accord this dispensation to persons whose night work ends around midnight when it is not possible for them to take their night meal before the hour of midnight." This is not possible under the wording of the indult accorded to the Ordinaries of the United States, except in the case wherein the work actually extends beyond the hour of midnight.

A further difference is found in the days on which this dispensation from the Eucharistic fast may be used. The indult granted to the United States permits its use on Sundays, feasts of obligation *and* one other day of the week. The Canadian indult permits its use on Sundays, feasts of precept *or* one other day of the week.

[48]"A dispensation . . . is an act of jurisdiction. Hence, dispensatory power may be exercised directly over subjects only. The following may be subjects in this matter: 'incolae'—inhabitants, whether in their own territory, or outside the same; 'advenae'—temporary residents, when they are staying in the territory of their quasidomicile; 'peregrini'—transients, with respect to general laws, since canon 14, § 1, states that they are not held to the observance of particular laws (see also canon 1313, 1°); 'vagi'—wanderers, when they are actually staying in a certain place (canon 14, § 2); the Superior himself, as also the person to whom he has granted *general* dispensatory power, for canon 201, § 3, states: Unless the nature of things or the law forbid, the non-judicial or so-called voluntary jurisdiction can be exercised even in one's own favor, and used outside the territory."—Cicognani, *Canon Law* (2. revised edition, Westminster, Md.: The Newman Bookshop, 1934) p. 834, n. 2.

[49]It will devolve upon each ordinary to select those methods of procedure which he considers best suited to his diocese and local circumstances. Thus, the Most Reverend Archbishop of Cincinnati, in a letter to the priests of his jurisdiction, under date of Nov. 13, 1946, directed that each individual application for this dispensation be submitted to the Chancery with the recommendation of the pastor. In the diocese of Rockford, the same method of procedure is required. His Eminence, the Most Reverend Archbishop of Philadelphia, on the other hand, extended the power to dispense to all the priests, diocesan and religious, under his jurisdiction, adding that as often as the faculty is used, a notice to that effect must be filed with the Chancery Office.

Before undertaking a discussion of the various difficulties which one meets in the interpretation of the indult, one may well seek to determine its precise purpose. For unless a person keeps before his mind the broadly expressed intention of the Holy See in this matter, he is likely to find himself unable to formulate a clear principle of action.

While frequent Communion is not mentioned in so many words, it is clearly implied in the indult by the nature of the grant. According to the common consensus of canonists and moral theologians, frequent Communion consists in the reception of the Holy Eucharist two or three times (*pluries*) a week.[50] The indult presently being considered grants the power to dispense night workers from the Eucharistic fast just twice a week (except for Holy Days of Obligation), the minimum number of Communions required to establish a person in the accepted category of frequent communicants. Hence it seems logical to conclude that the Holy See intends, by this indult, to make a practice of frequent Communion possible and convenient for those who habitually labor after midnight.

This conclusion is further indicated by the explicit mention of *daily* Communion in relation to a dispensation made available for Nursing Sisters. If, therefore, it is assumed that the indult has as its explicit purpose the encouraging of frequent Communion among night workers, and of daily Communion among Nursing Sisters who must work after midnight, it is possible to reason to a logical solution of most of the difficulties which present themselves.

Setting aside for a moment any consideration of the Nursing Sisters, the first question that arises concerns the free or non-working days (nights) of the dispensed night worker. With the night work considered on a weekly basis—for that is the minimum period of time in which the indult would be theoretically applicable—could the worker use the dispensation on those days when he did not work after midnight, and could he be licitly dispensed, in view of canon 84, if he had two days out of the week on which he could

[50]Cappello, *De Eucharistia,* p. 507; Gasparri, *Tractatus Canonicus de Sanctissima Eucharistia* (2 vols., Paris: Delhomme et Briguet, 1897), I, 369 (hereafter cited *De Sanctissima Eucharistia*).

conveniently communicate upon keeping the usual fast from midnight?

It seems safe to say that one or two non-working nights a week would not destroy the note of habituality as demanded in the indult, for in the United States a five-day working week is more the rule than the exception. Aside from the broad interpretation that is indicated in canon 68 for privileges whenever factors of doubt obtain in a case, it would constitute an undue restriction of the indult to limit its use to the exceptional worker whose occupation engages him in a six or seven day week. The indult would still be of advantage to the worker even if he chose to observe the fast on his two free days, for Communion on a third day of the week would still be within the concept of frequent Holy Communion which the indult evidently intends to encourage. However, it is the present writer's opinion that a worker who works as a rule only four nights a week could not licitly be dispensed under the indult. For if the broadest interpretation of frequent Communion is accepted to include the reception of Holy Communion three times a week, the dispensation would scarcely be justified in a case wherein the worker had three days on which he did not work after midnight and on which he could easily have observed the usual fast if he wished to communicate.

However, in the case of a person who works at least five nights out of the week, there is nothing stated or implied in the indult, aside from the obligation of avoiding scandal, which would require that the dispensation be applied only when the worker has labored the previous night. Hence the man or woman who works a five day week and has Friday and Saturday nights free could still use the privilege of communicating non-fasting on Sunday and on one other day of the week; and, needless to say, could still receive Holy Communion as many days beyond the two as he or she desired if the regular fast from midnight be observed.

It is, of course, within the right of the ordinary to limit the use of the dispensation to days on which the petitioner has worked the previous night. This conclusion is warranted in view of the fact that the ordinary is charged with the obligation of taking such precautions as he deems necessary to avoid scandal. If, then, in the judgment of the ordinary, scandal or even undue wonderment would be likely to result from the use of their privilege by dispensed workers on days not preceded by a night's work, a restriction of the privilege to days on which the previous night was spent in work would be demanded. However, if no such restriction is ordered by the ordinary, the worker would be perfectly free to use his dispensation even exclusively on days not preceded by work after midnight.

Another practical problem likely to arise in the application of the indult concerns those workers who labor after midnight only one week out of every two or three. During the remainder of the time they are employed on a day time or early evening shift. May such workers be classified as habitually working after midnight, or does the fact of their working an equal or even greater amount of the time during the day disqualify them under the indult?

Any attempt to solve this problem on a purely mathematical basis inevitably leads to a solution based on personal feelings in the matter. There is no mathematical norm by which one can establish the number of times an act must be repeated to constitute habituality, for it can just as well and correctly be said that a person habitually spends his winters in Florida as it can be said that he habitually smokes cigars. It seems better to approach the problem again with a view to the indult's purpose and the intention of the petitioner.

If, as the present approach postulates, the purpose of the indult is to foster the practice of frequent Communion among night workers, it should be made available to all those night workers who are impeded by their work from receiving Holy Communion at least two or three times a week as a regular practice. This practice will, of course, admit of occasional interruption without destroying or seriously impairing the concept of frequent Communion. However, it seems to the present writer that the indult is intended to include those workers whose practice of frequent Communion would be interrupted by their night work with some degree of regularity and to some serious extent. Again it is difficult to agree on the mathematical percentage necessary to constitute a serious interruption, but surely to be impeded in a practice even one fourth of the time gravely impairs the value and efficaciousness of the practice.

Thus, by considering the object of the indult to be Communion two or three times a week as a regular practice, and the habitual recurrence of work after midnight the obstacle to be removed by the dispensation, one can logically include those who work only one week out of every two or three. Instead of attempting to extend the meaning of "*habitualiter post mediam noctem laborantes*" to include these people, it is simply said that the habitual recurrence of their night work constitutes a serious impediment to their practice of frequent Communion.

However, it is important to note that this interpretation visualizes the worker as "habitually working after midnight" only during those weeks in which he actually does work after midnight. In other words, instead of the worker being placed in the category of those who continuously and practically without interruption work on the shift after midnight, his periodic weeks of work after midnight have been abstracted from chronology and considered a period of time in themselves during which the dispensation would validly and licitly apply. Hence, when a dispensation is given to such a worker, it should be made clear that it applies to those weeks only, and that it cannot be used during the remaining weeks in which he works on the day shift.

In considering the petitioner's request for a dispensation one should ascertain whether he intends to accept employment involving the regular recurrence of night work as a steady occupation, or whether it is merely a temporary position. On the basis of his answer, the bishop or the latter's delegate will be able to judge whether the petitioner's intended practice of frequent Communion would suffer more than an occasional interruption. If in the grantor's judgment the employment would not last long enough to constitute a reasonably serious interruption of the petitioner's practice of frequent Communion, it seems that the dispensation could not licitly be granted within the purpose of the indult and the requirements of canon 84. Needless to say, if, contrary to the intention of the petitioner, the employment proved of shorter duration than anticipated, it would have no retroactive effect on the dispensation's validity or licitness. The dispensation would simply cease in accordance with canon 86. In such a case a new dispensation would be required if another job involving night work were acquired.

In the case of a person who has been granted an unqualified dispensation in view of the continuous nature of his work after midnight, what is to be said if he suffers a temporary lay-off of two or three weeks? Is the dispensation temporarily suspended, or may he use it even though he is not working at all, or if he has accepted temporary day-time employment until his regular job resumes?

Assuming that the grantor has made no special provisions, such as setting the condition that the previous night be spent in work,[51] one may conclude that the temporary lay-off seems not to affect the continued available use of the dispensation. For there has been no total and certain cessation of the final cause, as canon 86 postulates for the non-applicability of the dispensation, but only a temporary suspension of it. And since the worker has been given an unqualified dispensation, he could, if he so desired, make use of it during those few weeks of temporary day employment. Neither would it be necessary for the worker to secure a new dispensation once his night work resumed, even though he may have accepted a totally different job on a temporary basis. His intention, in this case, would preserve a moral continuity in his chosen occupation.

The indult makes a further concession in favor of Nursing Sisters: "furthermore, in the case of Nursing Sisters dispensation may be granted for *daily* Communion whenever the previous night has been spent in the service of the sick."[52] Considered in its context, this concession must be understood to refer to the fre-

[51]Cf. *supra*, p. 81.

[52]This favor was extended to include religious brothers who act as nurses or infirmarians. "Letter of the Most Reverend Apostolic Delegate"—The Jurist, VII (1947), 339.

quency with which the dispensation may be used, and not as constituting an entirely different set of conditions for Nursing Sisters. The concession is, in the first place, given as a modification of a condition under which the general indult may be used. It is, furthermore, grammatically a part of the very sentence which restricts the use of the dispensation to Sundays and Feasts of Precept and for one other day during the week. Hence, it would be straining all rules of interpretation to consider the case of Nursing Sisters as not subject to all the general conditions of the indult. It appears, therefore, that the same line of reasoning that was offered above in relation to the faithful in general must be applied to Nursing Sisters as well. From this it follows that the indult does not envision the case of the Nursing Sisters who occasionally spend a night in the service of the sick, but rather of those sisters who habitually or according to a regular schedule do so.[53]

The fact, however, that the indult's purpose, in the case of Nursing Sisters, is to encourage *daily Communion,* as distinguished from *frequent* Communion in the case of the faithful, does necessitate a change in the number of nights during the week she must work after midnight in order to be licitly dispensed. It has been suggested above[54] that the worker as a rule should be employed at least five days a week after midnight in order to supply the just and reasonable cause for the dispensation as demanded by canon 84. The reason is that the worker could easily practice *frequent* Communion without any need of the dispensation if he had available more than two days not preceded by night work. *Daily* Communion, however, could not be practiced conveniently without the use of the dispensation unless he had a minimum of five days not preceded by work after midnight. This is based on the commonly accepted principle that one could abstain from Communion once

[53]The style of the Sacred Congregation indicates, however, that its intention may have been more liberal than its words. In the indult given to the Ordinaries of Canada it is quite clear that a Nursing Sister could be validly and licitly dispensed each time that she performs night service with the sick, provided, of course, that this be in a hospital. For there is nothing in the indult requiring that any of those eligible for dispensation be *habitually* engaged in the night service of the sick. Cf. *supra,* p. 78, footnote 47.

[54]*Supra,* p. 81.

or twice a week and still be considered a *daily* communicant.[55] Hence, in the case of the Nursing Sisters, a just and reasonable cause would exist for the granting of the dispensation whenever more than two nights in a week were spent in the service of the sick.

It is important to note that the Nursing Sisters may use their dispensation only on days preceded by work after the previous midnight. This is a restriction not placed on the faithful who have been dispensed for *frequent* Communion, and who may lawfully use the dispensation on Sundays, on feasts of obligation and on any one day of the week they choose, even though it be not preceded by work after midnight.[56]

Article 4. The Number of Times *per diem*

Just as the Church has declared the minimum number of times one must receive during a year, so it has wisely declared the maximum number of times one may receive in one day. Prior to the present Code of Canon Law there was no explicit canon which forbade the reception of Holy Communion oftener than once a day,[57] but the prohibition was universally deduced from the law which forbade the celebration of Mass more than once a day. It was the general teaching of the moralists, with which the Church concurred in its common practice, that the reception of Holy Communion, whether sacrificial or non-sacrificial, oftener than once in the same day was forbidden under pain of grave sacrilege.

The Code has incorporated such a prohibition in canon 857: *Nemini liceat sanctissimam Eucharistiam recipere, qui eam eadem die iam receperit, nisi in casibus de quibus in can. 858, § 1.* The cases referred to by canon 858, § 1, are the reception of Holy Viaticum in danger of death, and the necessity of consuming the Sacred Species in order to prevent their likely subjection to irreverence or desecration.

[55]Cappello, *De Eucharistia,* p. 507; Gasparri, *De Sanctissima Eucharistia,* II, 369.

[56]*Supra,* p. 81.

[57]Gasparri, *op. cit.,* II, 359.

Before the Code specifically indicated these two exceptions wherein the ecclesiastical law gives way to the divine law, authors disputed the point[58] whether or not Holy Viaticum should be administered to one who, having received Holy Communion earlier that day, was beset by a true danger of death. The question was settled beyond further dispute by the enactment of canon 864, § 2, of the Code, which not only permits but urges that Holy Viaticum be administered in such cases. Paragraph 3 of the same canon, however, implicitly indicates that Holy Viaticum should not be administered to the same person more than once in a single day.

ARTICLE 5. THE LITURGICAL RITE AND THE RECEPTION OF HOLY COMMUNION

A brief examination of the history of the discipline regarding the liturgical rite in which one may receive Holy Communion will serve as another example of the Church's more recent moves to encourage the frequent reception of Holy Communion.

As late as May 26, 1742, Pope Benedict XIV, in the Constitution, *Etsi pastoralis,* explicitly forbade Catholics of the Latin rite to receive Holy Communion under the species of leavened bread from priests of the Greek rite. Catholics of the Greek rite, however, were permitted to receive under the species of unleavened bread from Latin priests in places where there was no church of their own rite.[59]

In 1893, Pope Leo XIII relaxed this discipline to the extent of permitting the faithful of any rite, Latin or Oriental, in places where there existed no church or priest of their own rite, to receive Holy Communion, not only in danger of death and in the fulfillment of their Paschal duty, but even for the sake of their own devotion, according to the rite of the church existing in that place, provided that it was a Catholic church.[60] About a year later the same Pope extended this concession to Catholics of those places where a church of their own rite existed, but where in consequence of the great distance of any church of their proper rite from their

[58]Cf. Gasparri, *op. cit.,* I, 357.
[59]§ VI, nn. XII-XIII—*Fontes,* n. 328.
[60]S.C. de Prop. Fide, 18 aug. 1893—*Fontes,* n. 4926.

homes some of the faithful were not able to go to it without grave inconvenience. Judgment regarding the gravity of the inconvenience was left to the local ordinary.[61]

Finally, on September 14, 1912, Pope Pius X, in the Constitution *Tradita ab antiquis,* granted permission to all the faithful of whatsoever rite to receive Holy Communion in any rite they chose, apart from any necessity or grave reason. The only exception was that the fulfillment of one's Paschal obligation was under strict obligation to be carried out in one's own rite.[62]

The present discipline, as enacted in canon 866 of the Code, is taken from the foregoing decree of Pope Pius X. There is this difference, however, that the Code merely urges, apart from any strict obligation, that the faithful fulfill their Paschal duty in their own rite, while the decree of Pius X made it of strict obligation. The Code also makes the reception of Holy Viaticum an exception to the general rule and states that, aside from a case of urgent necessity, it must be received in one's own rite.[63] Cappello gives two reasons for this exception: first, because the administration of Holy Viaticum belongs to one's own pastor, according to canon 850; secondly, because inasmuch as one's proper rite is determined through the first sacrament, namely Baptism, and thereby also his external Christian mode of life, so it is necessary that through the last sacraments, Holy Viaticum and Extreme Unction, one should openly and externally profess his affiliation to his own church and proper rite.[64]

The present discipline on the liturgical rite in which one may receive Holy Communion can be summarized thus:

1) Catholics of the Latin rite may freely receive in the rite of any of the Oriental Catholic Churches, and for so doing need no other reason than that of their own desire properly prompted by devotion and piety.

[61]Litt. Ap., *Orientalium,* 30 nov. 1894, n. II—*Fontes,* n. 627: *Collect.,* n. 1883.

[62]Nn. III-IV—*Fontes,* n. 698; *Acta Apostolicae Sedis,* Commentarium Officiale (Romae, 1909-), IV (1912), 615-616.

[63]Cf. Can. 851, §§ 1-2.

[64]Cappello, *De Eucharistia,* p. 494.

2) Catholics of any Oriental rite enjoy the same privilege with regard to Communion in the Latin rite.

3) One can fulfill his Paschal obligation by receiving Holy Communion in a rite other than his own, but in so doing he would act contrary to the expressed desire of the Church.

4) When in danger of death, one must receive Holy Viaticum in one's own rite, unless some urgent necessity for receiving in a different rite intervenes.

Article 6. The Time and Place for Receiving Holy Communion

The final restrictions placed by law on the reception of Holy Communion concern the proper time and the fitting place for Its distribution. The present law regarding the days on which Holy Communion may be distributed is very unrestrictive; there are only two days of the year on which exceptions from the general law exist. Paragraph 1 of canon 867 declares that it is lawful to distribute Holy Communion every day. Paragraph 2 limits the giving of Holy Communion on Good Friday to the sick who are in true danger of death, and are therefore *obliged* to receive Holy Viaticum. Hence, no one else, under any pretext, may receive Holy Communion on that day.[65] Paragraph 3 of canon 867 permits the faithful to receive on Holy Saturday, but only during the Mass or immediately after it is finished.[66]

[65] Cf. *Rituale Romanum*, tit. IV, c. 2, n. 16.

[66] Although it is not explicitly stated, a prohibition against giving Holy Communion to others than the sick who are in danger of death on Holy Thursday after the solemn office is ended, that is, when the altar has been stripped and the ciborium has been removed to another place, is implied by the rubrics of the *Roman Missal*, which direct that some consecrated hosts be preserved for the sick. In this regard Canon P. Durieux remarks in his work, *The Eucharist, Law and Practice* (translated from the French by Rev. Oliver Dolphin, Chicago: The Lakeside Press, 1926), p. 205, footnote 386, as follows: "This prescription, moreover, binds only *sub levi;* but if the rubrics are observed, the distribution of Holy Communion after the office is impossible. In churches where the solemn office is not held, the prohibition against distributing Holy Communion does not exist; however, it is more in conformity with the mind of the Church to abstain from doing so. To recall more vividly the memory of the Last Supper, the Church wishes that on this day there shall be but one consecration and only one Eucharistic banquet." Cf. also Vermeersch-Creusen, *Epitome,* II, 94, n. 136.

The normal time of the day for the distribution of Holy Communion follows the prescriptions of law for the celebration of Mass (canon 867, § 4), that is, from one hour before dawn until one hour after mid-day (canon 821). The law is, however, less strict for the distribution of Holy Communion than for the celebration of Mass, for the canon permits exceptions to the general law for any reasonable cause. Correlative to this concession is the obligation of pastors, stated in canon 467, § 1, to administer the sacraments to the faithful as often as they lawfully (*legitime*) ask for them. Hence, a parishioner who asks for Holy Communion outside of Mass cannot lawfully be refused if he has a reasonable—not necessarily grave—cause for doing so.

Canon Durieux remarks that a reasonable cause would be found in physical or moral impossibility, a contemplated journey, greater convenience, etc.; but that the further removed the Communion is from the normal time, the more important should be the excuse, v.g., if it is a question of giving Communion in the evening or during the course of the night. He further notes that it is preferable and more in keeping with the nature of the sacrifice to distribute the Holy Eucharist after the Communion of the priest ("it would be an abuse, states the Holy See, to give Communion immediately after the consecration"); but the Code does not require any special reason for giving Communion either before, or after, or outside the time of Mass.[67]

In reply to a complaint made by a bishop against certain religious communities of women who insisted upon the practice of receiving Communion outside of Mass without grave reason and to the serious inconvenience of their chaplains, the Sacred Congregation of Rites replied: "*Episcopus utatur iure suo*."[68] It seems evident from this response that the Sacred Congregation does not consider the practice to be prohibited by the Code or any of the approved liturgical books; neither did it consider it a matter serious enough to merit correction universally. The bishop, by reason of the norms stated in canons 335 and 336, § 2, has the power to

[67]*The Eucharist, Law and Practice*, pp. 205-206.

[68]S.R.C., 25 maii 1934—Bouscaren, *The Canon Law Digest*, II, 217.

correct practices which, in his judgment, are abûses of the law. Hence, if the practice of sisters demanding Holy Communion before Mass constituted a truly grave inconvenience to their chaplains or an evident abuse of their rights, he could enact corrective legislation for his own territory.

According to canon 869, Holy Communion can be distributed in any place where Mass can licitly be celebrated; that is, in any church or oratory set aside for divine worship, even though it be not blessed or consecrated (cann. 822 and 1196). The ordinary, however, can forbid the distribution of Holy Communion in private oratories for just reasons and in individual cases.

When, according to canon 822, §§ 3-4, a priest has the privilege of celebrating Mass on a portable altar in any respectable and becoming place, he may licitly distribute Holy Communion in that same place as often as he celebrates Mass there. Canon 846 permits any priest who privately[69] celebrates Mass to distribute Holy Communion immediately before, during, and immediately after his Mass, provided it has not been forbidden for a just cause and in a particular case by the ordinary of the place.[70] It is reasonable to deduce that a place rendered suitable for the celebration of Mass by the designation *per modum actus* in accord with canon 822, §§ 3-4, also qualifies *per modum actus* for the distribution of Holy Communion according to canon 869 as often as Mass is celebrated there.

In response to a question raised by the Bishop of Mondovi in Piedmont, the Cardinal Secretary of the Sacred Congregation of the Sacraments, in his officially published annotations, observed that by reason of canon 822, § 4, in mountainous places "in which hamlets or houses were scattered over the country a long distance

[69]Cappello, *De Eucharistia,* p. 288 "Verba, *si privatim celebrat,* ita intelligenda, ut excludatur missa siva solemnis sive cantata sive conventualis; et verba *proxime* ante et *statim post* ita intelligi debent, ut sacerdos iam indutus sacris vestibus Sacrificii possit communionem distribuere." Cf. Decreta Authentica, n. 4177. A negative answer was given to the following question: An sacerdos, sacris vestibus Sacrificii indutus, possit administrare Sacram Communionem, *data rationabili causa,* ante vel post Missam solemnem aut cantatam aut etiam conventualem, sicuti permittitur ante vel post Missam privatam?

[70]Durieux, *The Eucharist, Law and Practice,* p. 204.

from the church . . . if . . . the Ordinary of the place can, under the terms of the canon above cited, grant permission to celebrate Mass in the hall or a house, and if he indicates that he is willing to grant this permission, then, although in fact the celebration of the Mass, owing to the want of a priest, does not occur, it will be licit to distribute Holy Communion in that place."[71]

Hence it is clear that a place designated for the celebration of Mass in accordance with the norm of canon 822, § 4, could also be used for the distribution of Holy Communion *per modum actus,* and, for a grave cause, also outside of Mass. This does not seem to be applicable in the case of the priest who enjoys the privilege of the portable altar according to canon 822, §§ 2-3, for in this case it is the designation of the place for the celebration of the Mass that is left to the priest by way of a privilege. To extend the use of the privilege of designating the place for the celebration of Mass to include the designation of a place as suitable for the distribution of Holy Communion outside of Mass seems to imply an undue extension which is out of keeping with canon 67 regarding the interpretation of privileges.

In view of the explicit exclusion of bedrooms as fitting places for the celebration of Mass (can. 822, § 4) and the prohibition against distributing Holy Communion in places where Mass may not be celebrated, it is obviously by way of exception to the general rule that Holy Communion can be brought to the sick whose illness confines them to bed. Hence there seems to be no justification for the practice of giving Holy Communion to other members of the family who are in good health, but who wish to take advantage of the priest's visit to their home to receive Holy Communion. Even if Communion were to be given them in some room other than the bedroom, it would be illicit unless some circumstances such as those mentioned in the case of the Diocese of Mondovi in Piedmont existed. Even then, the permission of the ordinary would be required. Speaking of the ordinary's capacity to delegate to a priest the power which canon 822, § 4, accords the ordinary,

[71]S.C. de Sacr., *Montis Regalis in Pedemonte,* 5 ian. 1928—Bouscaren, *The Canon Law Digest,* I, 392.

Cardinal Jorio, in the same annotations cited above, remarked: ". . . in consideration of the gravity of the matter and the narrow limits within which this power is restricted, the Ordinary should not delegate it unless the person to whom he proposes to delegate it be of such prudence that it may be foreseen that he will not abuse the power. Besides, in the act of delegation it must be clearly explained *what constitutes a just and reasonable cause;* what cases are to be regarded as *extraordinary;* and that a grant of the permission for a certain case does not extend to another case, even though the same circumstances exist, but that the permission must be expressly renewed."[72] Evidently, then, a dispensation from the law is not to be given arbitrarily by any priest who may feel moved to give Holy Communion in a private house to the nurse attending the sick person, or to other members of the family who are in good health.

Canon 868 forbids the distribution of Holy Communion during Mass to persons who are so far removed from the altar that the priest would have to depart from the sight of the altar in order to administer the Holy Eucharist to them. This prohibition does not seem to imply that the giving of Holy Communion behind an architectural obstruction which cuts off all view of the altar from either end of the altar rail would be illicit.

[72]Bouscaren, *The Canon Law Digest,* I, 392-393.

CHAPTER VI

THE OBLIGATION OF ENCOURAGING THE FREQUENT RECEPTION OF HOLY COMMUNION

Article 1. The Obligation of Parish Priests, Confessors and Preachers

The faithful are to be encouraged to receive Holy Communion frequently, and even daily, according to the norms given in the decrees of the Apostolic See, and those who assist at Mass should be urged to receive the Most Blessed Eucharist not only spiritually but sacramentally with the proper dispositions (canon 863).

This canon of the present law has its roots in the decree of the Council of Trent in which the mind and desire of the Church was first officially expressed on the matter: "The holy Council wishes indeed that at each Mass the faithful who are present should communicate, not only in spiritual desire but also by the sacramental partaking of the Eucharist . . ."[1]

It is supported by the several later decrees of the Holy See to which it refers and, as such, becomes much stronger than its Tridentine forerunner. Viewed in the light of these decrees, it is much more than a mere legal exhortation; more than an expressed desire of the Church. It is a condemnation of all teachings and practices opposed to the practice of frequent and daily Communion. Moreover, it is directed against those priests and pastors who, God forbid, indiscriminately deny the faithful frequent Holy Communion by neglecting or by refusing to distribute the Most Blessed Sacrament except on Sundays and feasts of precept. It is, furthermore, directed against those confessors who demand of their penitents such purity of soul for frequent Holy Communion that they scarcely ever find a person worthy of frequent or daily Communion according to the norms they have arbitrarily established.[2]

[1]Sess. XXII, *de sacrificio missae*, c. 6; cf. Schroeder, *Canons and Decrees of The Council of Trent*, p. 147 for English translation here used.

[2]Cappello, *De Eucharistia*, p. 509.

Foremost among the decrees referred to in canon 863 is the Decree *Sacra Tridentina Synodus* of Pope Pius X, issued on December 20, 1905.[3] This decree, by force of its own words as expressed in number IX of its disciplinary section, remains the last word regarding frequent and daily Communion, and forbids further controversy concerning the dispositions necessary for frequent and daily Communion.[4] Hence it is of major importance in this study carefully to examine its enactments in order to determine the exact limits within which the parish priest, confessor and preacher are to exercise their duties of encouraging and directing the souls in their care. What has been set down in the two preceding chapters regarding the obligation of receiving Holy Communion and concerning the limitations of law relative to Its reception are to be understood as taken for granted in the following pages. Reference will be made to various pages of the preceding chapters as often as the present writer feels that it will be necessary or helpful.

The first enactment of the Decree *Sacra Tridentina Synodus* declares:

> "Frequent and daily Communion, as a thing most earnestly desired by Christ Our Lord and by the Catholic Church, should be open to all the faithful, of whatever rank and condition of life; so that no one who is in a state of grace, and who approaches the holy table with a right and devout intention, can lawfully be hindered therefrom."[5]

It will be noted that here, and in all other enactments of the decree, *frequent* Holy Communion and *daily* Holy Communion are treated as one and the same thing with regard to the discipline governing them. As has been remarked earlier,[6] the term *frequent* Holy Communion is applied to the practice of receiving several (i.e. two or three) times a week; *daily* Holy Communion, to the

[3] *Fontes,* n. 4326; *Collect.,* n. 2225.

[4] "Finally, after the publication of this decree, all ecclesiastical writers are to cease from contentious controversies concerning the dispositions requisite for frequent and daily Communion."—Decree *Sacra Tridentina Synodus,* n. IX.

[5] The translation of this excerpt from the Decree *Sacra Tridentina Synodus,* as well as all future excerpts of this decree herein employed, is taken from the translation originally furnished in the "London Tablet." Cf. *supra,* pp. 39-40.

[6] *Supra,* pp. 80 and 85.

practice of receiving every day, even though the reception of Holy Communion may be omitted one or two days of each week. The decree makes no distinction between the two practices. It requires no greater virtue for one than for the other, nor does it reserve the practice of one or the other to any particular group of the faithful. In using the two terms the decree simply recognizes the distinction employed by the earlier theologians; but in ignoring the practical importance of this distinction the decree recalls to mind the words of St. John Chrysostom: "Those who are worthy of receiving Holy Communion once a year should be worthy to receive daily; and if they are not, it were better that they abstain even from the annual Communion."[7]

Hence it is clear that confessors should refrain from requiring a greater degree of spiritual perfection for daily Communion than for frequent Communion. According to the decree, the judgment of anyone's worthiness or right to practice either frequent or daily Communion must be based, not on the person's condition and rank in life, but, *ceteris paribus,* solely on the state of his soul with regard to the state of grace or the state of mortal sin,[8] and on the presence or absence of a right and devout intention.

In number 2 of the disciplinary part of the decree, the "right intention" required for frequent and daily Communion is authoritatively defined:

> "A right intention consists in this: that he who approaches the holy table should do so, not out of routine or vain glory or human respect, but for the purpose of pleasing God, of being more closely united with Him by Charity, and of seeking this divine remedy for his weakness and defects."

This definition contains two elements: one negative and the other positive, and definitely states the only *necessary* elements of a "right intention." Negatively, it excludes the motives of routine, vain glory and human respect. To receive Holy Communion solely because "every one else does" or because it is the custom, or because

[7]*Supra,* p. 6—*De incomprehensibili Dei Natura, Homilia 6, De beato Philogonio—MPG,* XLVIII, 755.

[8]*Supra,* p. 40.

it makes others regard the communicant as pious and holy, or for any other purely human reason, would surely not constitute the right intention required by the decree. Positively, the decree declares that a person who, in receiving the Holy Eucharist, hopes thereby to please God, and to be more closely united to Him in Charity, or simply to obtain thereby a remedy for his weakness and defects has a right intention.

It is obvious, however, to anyone familiar with the principles of moral theology that those motives which do not suffice to constitute a right intention can sometimes be present in varying degrees without displacing or destroying the efficacy of a concomitant right intention. True, they may lessen the intensity of the right intention and even constitute venial sin, but their presence would not necessarily indicate the total lack of a right intention which could render the reception of Holy Communion unworthy and sacrilegious.[9]

It may also be noted that the right intention need not be more explicit than that required for any good act. An implicit intention suffices. And as, Cappello remarks, unless such an intention is positively and explicitly excluded, it is always presumed to be present at least implicitly and in some connected fashion.[10] While such an implicit intention is admittedly less perfect, in so far as it indicates a less perfect disposition of the mind in the recipient of Holy Communion, it is, nevertheless, sufficient, and no confessor could be justified in refusing frequent and daily Communion to a penitent confessing such a state of mind.

The next three paragraphs (nos. 3, 4 and 5) of the decree specify several *useful* and desirable conditions for the practice of frequent and daily Communion. Their separation from the *necessary conditions* is most clear, and they must never be exacted to such an extent that anyone would for the simple lack of their presence be turned away, or even discouraged, from frequent and daily Communion.

[9]Cf. Cappello, *De Eucharistia,* p. 514.

[10]*Loc. cit.*

Number 3 states:

"Although it is most expedient that those who communicate be free from venial sins, especially from such as are fully deliberate, and from any affection thereto; nevertheless it is sufficient that they be free from mortal sin, with [i.e. and that they have] the purpose of never sinning mortally in the future; and if they have this sincere purpose, it is impossible but that by daily Communion they should gradually emancipate themselves from even venial sins, and from all affection thereto."

It is most clear from the foregoing paragraph that the rules given by Lehmkuhl (1834-1918),[11] which had received the somewhat qualified approval of the Sacred Congregation for the Propagation of the Faith "as directions which in general could be given to confessors"[12] and represented the opinion of most of the theologians of that time[13] are altogether abolished as rules of necessity. As Cappello so pointedly remarks, the error of the older writers and doctors lay precisely in that they thought one disposition to be necessary for occasional (e.g., annual, monthly) Communion and another (more perfect) for frequent and daily Communion,[14] whereas in truth one and the same disposition, namely absence of mortal sin and a right intention, suffices for both. However, lest the Church seem to make light of venial sin and appear to countenance mediocrity in the spiritual life, the decree emphasizes the expediency and value of being free from such lesser sin in order that the fruits of Holy Communion may be more abundant. Hence, confessors and others charged with the care of souls in this matter are to encourage the complete conquering of venial sin and all affection thereto especially in frequent and daily communicants.

Paragraph number 4 points out the usefulness of improving the recipient's dispositions through suitable preparation for and thanksgiving after Holy Communion:

"But whereas the Sacraments of the New Law, though they [through the very fact of being administered to and

[11] Cf. *supra,* p. 36.

[12] Cf. *supra,* p. 37.

[13] *Loc. cit.*

[14] *De Eucharistia,* p. 512.

received by a duly qualified subject] take effect *ex opere operato,* nevertheless produte a greater effect in proportion as the dispositions of the recipient are better: therefore, care is to be taken that Holy Communion is preceded by serious preparation, and followed by a suitable thanksgiving according to each one's strength, circumstances, and duties."

Cappello has written that frequent and daily Communion is to be denied to those who *habitually* omit a serious preparation and suitable thanksgiving, duly accommodated to their proper aptitude with relation to the circumstances of their life and the duties of their state, on the grounds that they openly show that they do not approach the Holy Table with a right and pious intention, and therefore lack the necessary dispositions.[15]

The present writer is inclined to feel—*salva reverentia*—that Cappello is assuming too much when he concludes that habitual lack of preparation and thanksgiving furnishes patent proof of the absence of a right intention. The decree itself, it is true, cautions that the effects of the Sacrament are greater in proportion to the good qualities of the recipient's dispositions, and strongly urges serious preparation and thanksgiving as means toward improving the dispositions. On the other hand, it is most clear, from the mention that the effect of the sacrament follows *ex opere operato,* that the preparation and thanksgiving are not *necessary* elements of a right intention, but simply factors which produce a *better* disposition. Cappello clearly states this same principle on an earlier page of his work,[16] but later insists that *some* (*aliquis*) act of preparation and thanksgiving is required in view of the reverence which is due to so great a Sacrament, so that he who omits all preparation and thanksgiving cannot inherently on that score (*per se*) be excused from irreverence, or consequently from sin.

Even though this be true, still to the present writer it does not seem illogical to say that a person can receive Holy Communion frequently and even daily with at least an implicit intention

[15]*De Eucharistia,* p. 520.

[16]*Ibid,* p. 513.

of pleasing God and of attaining divine help in his struggles against sin, and at the same time be habitually neglectful with regard to preparation and thanksgiving. If Cappello meant to imply—which he does not state—that the irreverence consequent upon the lack of preparation and thanksgiving amounted, in truth, to a disdain for the Sacrament, then surely the subject should be denied *all* Communion until he remedy his sacrilegious attitude. But if the constant neglect of preparation and thanksgiving is occasioned by distraction or some other human weakness, then it is difficult to see how, in view of the explicit wording of the decree (no. 1), a confessor could lawfully deny the subject frequent and daily Communion.

This stand is not intended as minimizing in any way the importance of serious preparation for and thanksgiving after Holy Communion, but only as emphasizing what serious cause must exist and how clearly defined it must be, before anyone should be deterred from the practice of frequent or daily Communion.

The fifth paragraph of the decree advises:

> "That the practice of frequent and daily Communion be carried out with greater prudence and more abundant merit, the confessor's advice should be asked. Confessors, however, are to be careful not to dissuade anyone (*ne quemquam avertant*) from frequent and daily Communion, provided that he is in a state of grace, and approaches with a right intention."

Again this directive is not to be understood as a necessary condition for the practice of frequent and daily Communion. It is simply a recommendation made with a view of increasing the benefits to be derived from the practice. The advice of a confessor in the matter of frequent and daily Communion had been recommended in earlier decrees dealing with Holy Communion. The Decree *Cum ad aures* (1679), mentioned earlier in this treatise,[17] had entrusted the prescription of frequent Holy Communion almost entirely to the confessor who, "exploring the secrets of the heart, . . . would judge whether it [frequent Communion] would contribute to their salvation, and should accordingly prescribe it for

[17]Cf. *supra*, p. 28.

them." The Decree *Quemadmodum* (1890) confirmed this prerogative of confessors for religious institutes, strongly implying that the confessor's permission was required for the practice of frequent or daily Communion.[18]

It is evident from the Decree *Sacra Tridentina Synodus* that the directive authority of the confessor, whatever it may have been before the decree, is now strictly limited to giving judgment and counsel. In his capacity as judge, the confessor can declare a penitent to be unworthy of Communion in consequence of a lack of the state of grace or of the absence of a right intention. He may also in view of the particular factors attending a given case advise against the practice of frequent or daily Communion on the grounds that it would interfere with the penitent's duties toward his family, his work, etc.,[19] but he is strictly forbidden, from the viewpoint of a purely objective consideration, either directly or indirectly, to dissuade from the practice of frequent and daily Communion any person who is in a state of grace, and who approaches with a right intention, as explained above. The main burden of the confessor will be, according to the decree, to see to it that the frequent and even daily reception of Communion be practiced with "greater prudence and more abundant merit."

After listing the necessary conditions and the major factors of usefulness in relation to the frequent and daily reception of Holy Communion, the decree (no. 6) imposes the obligation of exhorting the faithful to adopt this praiseworthy practice on "parish priests, confessors, and preachers":

> "But since it is plain that, by frequent or daily reception of the Holy Eucharist, union with Christ is fostered, the spiritual life more abundantly sustained, the soul more richly endowed with virtues, and an even surer pledge of everlasting happiness bestowed on the recipient; therefore parish priests, confessors, and preachers—in accordance with the approved teachings of the *Roman Catechism* (part II, cap. 4, n. 63)—are frequently, and with great zeal, to exhort the faithful to this devout and salutary practice."

[18]Cf. *infra,* p. 106.

[19]Cappello, *De Eucharistia,* p. 518.

The seriousness of this obligation is emphasized by its studied repetition in subsequent decrees and enactments. On September 15, 1906, the Sacred Congregation of the Council,[20] in reply to various questions occasioned by the Decree *Sacra Tridentina Synodus,* published responses to two particular doubts concerning the extension of the words "*omnibus christifidelibus cuiusvis ordinis aut conditionis.*"

The first doubt concerned the admission of children to frequent and daily Communion. It was the custom in some dioceses, as the Sacred Congregation remarks,[21] to prohibit children from receiving the Holy Eucharist for as long as a year after their first Holy Communion. Hence the doubt was proposed: "Whether daily reception of the Eucharist should be urged on Catholic youths and even children after their first Holy Communion?"

After reviewing the arguments in favor of and against the proposed practice, the Sacred Congregation concluded as follows:

> "Frequency of Holy Communion is commended, according to the first article of the decree, also for children, who have been once admitted to the Holy Table according to the norms of the *Roman Catechism,* cap. 4, n. 63, and they should not be prohibited from its frequent participation, but rather exhorted to it, any custom existing to the contrary being hereby reprobated."

Later, in his Decree *Quam singulari,* issued on August 8, 1910, through the Sacred Congregation of the Sacraments,[22] Pope Pius X repeated the injunction, stating that "those who have charge of children must make every effort that the children, after their first Communion may approach the Holy Table frequently, and if possible even daily, as Christ and Mother Church desire, and that they do so with all the devotion of which they are capable at their age."[23]

[20]*Romana et aliarum—Fontes,* n. 4329.

[21]*Fontes,* n. 4329. Cf. *ibid.*, p. 836, *in fine.*

[22]*Fontes,* n. 2103; Denzinger, nn. 2137-2144; *AAS,* II (1910), 582-583.

[23]Cf. n. 6 of this decree.

As has already been seen, the Code has embodied this obligation in canon 863, expressly stating that the goal to be sought in this matter is that *all* when attending Mass should, if rightly disposed, sacramentally receive the Most Holy Eucharist.

The reserved Instruction on *Daily Communion and Precautions to Be Taken Against Abuses,* issued by the Sacred Congregation of the Sacraments on December 8, 1938, repeats the obligation in the following words:

> "This practice, a source of innumerable blessings, is not only to be commended but to be further propagated, and that, not only among the faithful in general, but also among young people and children, according to the precept imposed by the aforementioned decrees . . ."[24]

Still later, on July 14, 1941, the Sacred Congregation of the Council in an Instruction on *Exhorting the Faithful to Frequent and Devout Assistance at the Sacrifice of the Mass,* again stressed the obligation in an earnest exhortation that:

> "All Ordinaries everywhere in the world . . . personally and through pastors of souls and both secular and religious priests, . . . zealously instruct the faithful . . . in the rich blessings of sharing in the divine banquet as often as they are present at Mass, so that they may be more intimately united to Christ, as stated in the Decree of this Sacred Congregation of 20 Dec., 1905, *On the Daily Reception of the Most Blessed Eucharist,* and according to the teaching of the Council of Trent . . ."[25]

In view of this strong insistence on the part of the Holy See, it would be difficult for any priest charged with the care of souls to minimize the seriousness of his obligation to encourage frequent and daily Communion among his people. The Decree *Sacra Tridentina Synodus* demands that they exhort the faithful "frequently, and with great zeal."

The *Roman Catechism* is referred to in the decree as the source from which parish priests, confessors and preachers are to draw the approved teaching regarding the reception of the Holy

[24]Bouscaren, *The Canon Law Digest,* II, 208.

[25]Bouscaren, *The Canon Law Digest,* II, 359-360.

Eucharist. It is scarcely within the scope of the present work to include a detailed discussion of the dogmatic and moral principles therein contained, but in order to give the reader a general indication of what he may expect to find upon consultation of the work, the following brief summary is offered.

> The pastor will expound to all, indiscriminately and without reserve, the following truths regarding the salutary effects of this Sacrament:
>
> 1) The Eucharist is the fountain of all grace, containing as it does, after an admirable manner, the source of all gifts and graces, the author of all the Sacraments, Christ Our Lord, from whom as from their source they derive all their goodness and perfection.
>
> 2) The symbols of this Sacrament, bread and wine, indicate what the Body and Blood of Christ are, in a superior manner to the health and joy of the soul. But, it is not, like bread and wine, changed into our substance; but in some measure, changes us into its own nature.
>
> 3) This Sacrament imparts grace. It is beyond all doubt that those who piously and religiously receive this Sacrament receive the Son of God in their souls, and are united, as living members, to His body.
>
> 4) To communicate worthily, it is necessary that the recipient be in the state of grace.
>
> 5) There can be no doubt that the Eucharist remits venial sin.
>
> 6) The Holy Eucharist is an antidote against the contagion of sin, and a shield against the violent assaults of temptation.
>
> 7) It is a remedy against the concupiscence of the flesh.
>
> 8) The Holy Eucharist facilitates, in a wonderful manner, the attainment of eternal life.
>
> 9) These truths are to be found in the sixth chapter of St. John's Gospel.
>
> 10) There are to be distinguished three possible manners relative to the act of communicating:
>
> > a) The exclusively sacramental reception, which exists on the part of those who receive the Most Holy Eucharist either while they are in the state of mortal sin or when they approach the Holy Table without the requisite proper intention;
> >
> > b) The purely spiritual reception, which exists on the part of those who, inspired and inflamed with a lively faith,

participate of the Celestial Food in and through their earnest desire for it;

c) The simultaneously sacramental and spiritual reception, which exists on the part of those who in act as well as in desire approach the Holy Table in a worthy state and with a commendable intention.

11) Some preparation is necessary relative to the act of sacramental Communion if it is to prove useful and advantageous to the recipient. Six steps toward a completely satisfactory preparation are indicated:

a) "Distinguish table from table," that is, elicit an act of faith in the Divine Presence in the Holy Eucharist.

b) Remove any impediment to grace by forgiving and being reconciled with your neighbors, if there be any necessity for it.

c) Examine your consciences, and receive sacramental absolution if need be.

d) Acknowledge your unworthiness to receive.

e) Elicit an act of the love of God.

f) Be prepared in body by fasting from midnight.[26]

12) The Paschal Precept binds as a grave obligation.[27]

13) The practice of the frequent reception of Holy Communion is a matter of profound importance.

14) All baptized persons who have reached the years of discretion are subject to the precept of annual Communion.

15) It is the burden of parents and confessors to determine the age of discretion in children, and to ascertain when they are ready to make their first Holy Communion.[28]

Article 2. The Obligation of Superiors of Religious Orders and Congregations

Superiors shall promote frequent and even daily reception of the Most Sacred Body of Christ among their subjects; frequent and

[26]Other recommendations regarding the physical preparation for Holy Communion are mentioned in the Catechism, in regard to which cf. Cappello, *De Eucharistia*, pp. 486-493, *passim*.

[27]The *Catechism* mentions the sentence of excommunication to be incurred by those who are remiss in this matter. As has been mentioned previously (*supra*, p. 50), this penalty has since been abrogated by the Code.

[28]*The Catechism of the Council of Trent*, Published by command of Pope Pius V, translated into English by the Rev. J. Donovan, (New York: The Catholic Publication Society, 1829), pp. 164-171.

daily access to the Most Holy Eucharist is to be freely permitted to religious who are rightly disposed (canon 595, § 2).

It is clear from this canon of the Code that all superiors of religious, whether they preside in orders or in congregations[29] of men or of women,[30] are to promote frequent and daily Communion among their subjects. This canon is taken substantially from number 7 of the Decree *Sacra Tridentina Synodus,* which reads in part[31] as follows:

> "Frequent and daily Communion is to be promoted especially in religious orders and congregations of all kinds; with regard to which, however, the Decree *Quemadmodum* issued on December 17, 1890, by the Sacred Congregation of Bishops and Regulars is to remain in force."

The pertinent parts of the Decree *Quemadmodum* referred to by the Decree *Sacra Tridentina Synodus* are contained in the Code under canon 595, §§ 3-4:

> § 3—"If, however, a religious has since the last confession given grave scandal to the community, or has committed an external mortal sin, the superior can forbid that religious to receive Holy Communion until he (or she) has again made a sacramental confession.
>
> § 4—"If the rules or constitutions, or also the calendars, of any religious organization, whether of simple or of solemn vows, prescribe certain fixed days for the reception of Holy Communion, they shall have a merely directive force."

In so far as the Decree *Quemadmodum* remains in force by reason of the Decree *Sacra Tridentina Synodus,* and retains a binding force in accord also with the norms of canon 6, 2°, 3°, 4°, it seems necessary to mention whatever changes were effected in it by the new legislation. Number V of the Decree *Quemadmodum* reads as follows:

> "In so far as the permission for or prohibition of receiving Holy Communion is concerned, His Holiness Leo XIII decrees and orders that permissions or prohibitions of this kind pertain solely to the ordinary or extraordinary confessor, and that

[29]Can. 488, 1° and 7°.

[30]Can. 490.

[31]It also speaks of the obligation incumbent on the heads of seminaries. Cf. *infra*, pp. 110-111.

superiors have no authority whatsoever to interfere in this matter, except in the case in which one of their subjects has given scandal to the community, or has committed some notoriously grave sin since his last sacramental confession. In such a case the superior may enforce a prohibition until the delinquent has approached the sacrament of penance."[32]

It is to be noted that the authority conceded to the confessor in this decree, namely, to permit or to prohibit the reception of Holy Communion, is now strictly defined by the Decree *Sacra Tridentina Synodus.* He may not, under any circumstances, demand of a religious a greater state of spiritual perfection for frequent and daily Communion than is required by the decree for anyone, namely, the state of grace and a right intention. This has been defined beyond all doubt in Number 1 of the Decree *Sacra Tridentina Synodus.*

Regarding the extraordinary case in which a superior can prohibit a subject from receiving Holy Communion, the Code has incorporated substantially the law as given in the Decree *Quemadmodum.* The Code, however, has added the adjective *grave* to the word *scandalum,* which alone was employed in the decree. This addition was evidently made with a view of forestalling possible abuses of this power on the part of over-zealous superiors. The word "scandal" has been given a very wide extension in meaning by modern usage, and is often interpreted to denote actions or words which are only shocking or surprising. Although the Code uses the disjunctive "*aut*" between the phrases "*gravi scandalo*" and "*gravem externam culpam,*" the context of canon 595, § 3, leads one to conclude that the scandal there spoken of must be considered as a matter of most serious detrimental import and as equivalent, if not in actual fact, at least in potential effect, to the demoralizing influence of a notoriously grave sin openly committed.

The fact of notoriety postulated in such a case is also worthy of mention. In the case of a prohibition against the reception of Communion which would entail scandal, the canon postulates that the community, and not just some members of the community, be

[32]*Fontes,* n. 2017; *ASS,* XXIII (1890-1891), 507.

affected, at least indirectly. Thus, if scandal were given to only one or two members of a fairly large community, and no grave external sin was involved in the case, the superior would exceed his or her right in forbidding the guilty member to receive Holy Communion. This restriction of the superior rests on the principle that the confessor alone is the judge of one's worthiness to receive Holy Communion as long as the good of the community is not seriously involved.

Number 6 of the Decree *Quemadmodum* has been affected substantially by the subsequent legislation. However, an examination of it may be useful for the purpose of emphasizing by contrast the scope of the present legislation. It reads as follows:

> "Hence all are advised to take diligent care in preparing themselves for and in receiving Holy Communion on the days specified by their rules; and as often as the confessor shall judge that the fervor and spiritual progress of an individual warrants a more frequent reception, the same confessor may permit it. But he who obtains permission from his confessor for a more frequent and even the daily reception of Holy Communion is bound to inform his superior of this; and if the superior thinks he has just and grave causes for opposing the more frequent reception of Holy Communion, he is bound to manifest them to the confessor, whose judgment must always be acquiesced in."[33]

The first effect of this decree was to abrogate those rules or statutes in the constitutions of religious orders and congregations which limited the reception of Holy Communion to certain fixed days.[34] Later this same ruling was incorporated by the Sacred Congregation of Bishops and Regulars in its *Normae* for approving the constitutions of new institutes of simple vows.[35] Article 151 of these *Normae* provided that any rule that appointed certain days on which members of these congregations are required to receive Holy Communion are not to be considered as a refusal to allow them to approach the Holy Table on other days also.

[33] *Fontes*, n. 2017; *ASS*, XXIII (1890-1891), p. 507.

[34] Cf. Response to *Dubia circa decretum "Quemadmodum,"* 17 aug. 1891--*ASS*, XXV (1892-1893), 109-111.

[35] *Normae secundum quas S. Cong. Ep. et Reg. procedere solet in approbandis novis institutis votorum simplicium*, p. 28.

Number 8 of the Decree *Sacra Tridentina Synodus* provides a similar directive, but makes it more clear that there is no obligation to receive Holy Communion even on the days appointed by the constitutions or other rules:

> "In the case of religious institutes, whether of solemn or of simple vows, in whose rules, or constitutions, or calendars, Communion is assigned to certain fixed days, such regulations are to be regarded as *directive* and not *preceptive*. In such cases the appointed number of Communions should be regarded as a minimum, and not as setting a limit to the devotion of the religious."

The Code has incorporated the first sentence of this decree almost verbatim in canon 595, § 4, as quoted above.

A further change effected in Number 6 of the Decree *Quemadmodum* by subsequent legislation concerns the authority of the confessor. The decree apparently sanctioned the right of the confessor to judge whether the fervor and spiritual progress of an individual warranted a more frequent reception of Holy Communion, and to permit it if he saw fit. As has been remarked previously, in consequence of the provisions of the Decree *Sacra Tridentina Synodus,* the confessor no longer enjoys this authority in the event that the subject is in the state of grace and has a right intention. It follows from the abrogation of this authority, and from the consequent absence of any need to secure the permission of the confessor for the frequent or daily reception of Holy Communion, that the religious subject need not inform the superior of his or her intention to receive frequently or daily. Hence, the former obligation of duly informing the superior, as it was enacted in the Decree *Quemadmodum,* is no longer in force.

The obligation of religious superiors to encourage frequent and daily Communion among their subjects rests solidly on the aforementioned laws and decrees. It is true that much of the legislation is negative in its nature, in so far as it restricts the superior's possible inclination to interfere with his or her subject's devotional desires. In order to forestall every subterfuge, and also to preclude all likely emergence of Jansenistic practices contrary to the law and the decrees, the Decree *Sacra Tridentina Synodus* ordered the annual public reading of its enactments to all religious subjects:

> "Therefore, freedom of access to the Eucharistic table, whether more frequently or daily, must always be allowed them, according to the principles above laid down in this decree. And in order that all religious of both sexes may clearly understand the provisions of this decree, the superior of each house is to see to it that it is read in community, in the vernacular, every year, within the octave of the feast of Corpus Christi."[36]

Number 8 of the Decree *Quemadmodum* had likewise insisted that that decree be publicly read to the community at least once a year at a given time.[37] However, since the promulgation of the Code of Canon Law these prescriptions are no longer in force.[38]

Article 3. Special Obligations with Regard to Children and Young People

The various decrees and responses of the Holy See regarding frequent and daily Communion have so emphasized its desire that the frequent reception of Holy Communion be promoted among children and young people, that a separate treatment of the question seems warranted in this place. While there are involved special difficulties which demand certain precautionary measures as indicated by the Holy See, these will be treated in a later chapter concerning the forestalling of abuses in connection with the practice of promoting the frequent and daily reception of Communion. The purpose of the present article is to establish the obligation, incumbent on all who are entrusted with the spiritual care of the young, of promoting the frequent and daily reception of Communion among them.

Seminaries enjoy special mention in the Decree *Sacra Tridentina Synodus* where it speaks of fostering frequent and daily Com-

[36]No. 8, *in fine*.

[37]Cf. *Fontes*, n. 2017.

[38]Cf. Schaefer, *De Religiosis ad Normam Codicis Iuris Canonicis* (ed. 3., Roma: S.A.L.E.R. Roppresentante della casa editrice Herder, 1940), p. 704.

munion in Christian institutions for the training of youth.[39] This obligation was spoken of in the Council of Trent (1545-1563) in the decree which placed on the bishops of dioceses the obligation of surveillance over their seminaries. It was made the duty of the bishop to see to it that the seminarians attended Mass daily, received the Sacrament of Penance at least once a month, and received Holy Communion as often as the judgment of the confessor allowed.[40]

The Code of Canon Law has incorporated the substance of this law in canon 1367, having reworded it to fit the discipline of the decree *Sacra Tridentina Synodus*. The bishop is still charged with the obligation, but the role of the confessor is not mentioned. The seminarian, according to the canon, is to receive the Holy Eucharist frequently with all due devotion and piety.[41]

There is no other explicit universal legislation as known to the present writer, which is directly concerned with seminarians and frequent Holy Communion, except that which concerns the possible abuses which must be forestalled. The treatment of that matter will follow in its proper place. But the lack of copious directives and exhortation does not in any way minimize the seriousness of the obligation. If anything, it points perhaps to the fact that there is little need of urging what already exists in practice. It is but natural that frequent and daily Communion would be widely practiced in seminaries; but if, in any place, the desires of the Holy See in this matter have not been fulfilled, then it is clear that the bishop of the place is charged with the obligation of applying to his seminarians, through the rector and the spiritual director, what has been said in the foregoing pages regarding the practice of frequent and daily Communion, and what will now be considered in relation to It as affecting all young people in general, since whatever applies

[39]No. 7: "Frequent and daily Communion is to be promoted . . . especially in ecclesiastical seminaries, where students are preparing for the service of the altar; . . ." *Fontes,* n. 4326.

[40]"Curet Episcopus ut singulis diebus missae sacrificio intersint, ac saltem singulis mensibus confiteantur peccata, et juxta confessoris judicium sumant corpus domini nostri Jesu Christi."—Sess. XXIII, *de ref.,* c. 18.

[41]"Curent Episcopi ut alumni Seminarii: . . . frequenter, qua par est pietate, Eucharistico pane se reficiant."—Can. 1367, 2°.

to them, applies *a fortiori* to seminarians in double measure in view of their high calling.

The Decree *Sacra Tridentina Synodus* laid down the rule that

> "Frequent and daily Communion . . . must be promoted as much as possible in seminaries, where students are preparing for the service of the altar; as also in all Christian establishments, of whatever kind, for the training of youth."[42]

The Decree *Quam singulari* ruled that

> "Those who have charge of children must make every effort that the children, after their first Communion, may approach the Holy Table frequently, and if possible daily, as Christ and Mother Church desire, and that they do so with all the devotion of which they are capable at their age."[43]

The same decree, in another place, named specifically those whom it intended to bind by this obligation; namely, parents, confessors, teachers and pastors.[44]

In an Instruction to the members of the Priests' Eucharistic League, approved by Pope Pius X on July 27, 1906, the members are directed in the following words:

> "They will take particular pains to excite a lively desire for daily Communion in the hearts of children, which are innocent and free from *vain fears,* when preparing them for First Communion as soon as they are capable, and as far as possible get them to renew this desire day by day."[45]

Finally, there is the answer of the Sacred Congregation of the Council of September 15, 1906:

> "Frequency of Holy Communion is commended, also for children, who have been once admitted to the Holy Table according to the norms of the Roman Catechism, cap. 4, n. 63, and they should not be prohibited from its frequent participation, but rather exhorted to it, any custom existing to the contrary being hereby reprobated."[46]

[42]No. 7—*Fontes,* n. 4326.

[43]No. 6—*AAS,* II (1910), 582; *Fontes,* n. 2103.

[44]*Ibid.,* no. 4.

[45]*Emmanuel,* XII (1906), 208.

[46]*Fontes,* n. 4329.

In the face of these explicit recommendations, no one could call into question the propriety and obligation of urging frequent and daily Communion among children. It is clearly the wish and the command of the Holy See that this be done. The extent to which parents, confessors, teachers and pastors share this obligation would be difficult, if not impossible, to define. But that is of small importance. Each is bound in proportion to his natural share in the formation of the child's spiritual and religious habits. Pastors are bound by the very fact that the spiritual care of all souls in their parishes is entrusted to them; confessors, by their office as judge, counsellor and physician of the souls that are freely and confidently opened to them. Among teachers, those especially who teach in academies, colleges and other establishments in which students live both night and day, are obliged to fulfill the duties of parents in this matter. They must not only remove all obstacles which an ill-adapted curriculum might offer, but must promote in a positive way, with proper precautions,[47] the practice of frequent and daily Holy Communion.

As for those children who remain in the care of their parents, the obligation founded on the natural law and declared in the Decree *Quam singulari,* has been well stated by the writer who said:

> "All the zeal of the pastor is marred unless the parents also do their part. They are bound, at least, to do two things. First, they must see that the children attend the special instructions which are given to first communicants. Is it not very hard upon the priest, and a proof of great indifference to Almighty God when children are allowed by their parents persistently to stay away from and to neglect that very instruction which is especially intended to make them less unworthy and less unprepared for this, one of the greatest events of their lives? . . . In the second place comes the wider and more difficult duty of training up the child in piety and spiritual feeling, so that when our Lord comes, He may come to a heart that is truly able to give Him a welcome and an abiding dwelling place."[48]

[47]Cf. *infra*, pp. 127 ff.

[48]Loyola, "The Preparation of Children for First Communion"—*Emmanuel,* XX (1914), 215.

It is not enough then, to simply fulfill the obligation which is enacted in canon 860, namely, of seeing to it that children and young people fulfill the Paschal Precept.[49] The decrees are clear in their insistence on frequent and daily Communion for the young. This is to be accomplished not only through instruction and good example, but by forming in the child the desire and habitual dispositions necessary for the reception of Holy Communion. As has been so aptly expressed:

> "If parent and teachers cooperate, the desire of Communion will be born in these young souls, the grace of God will develop it. But we must second this divine work, we must wage war on sin and evil inclinations, we must teach the children to overcome their budding passions, to correct faults which they know our Lord will not like to find in their hearts when He comes."[50]

[49]"Obligatio praecepti communionis sumendae, quae impuberes gravat, in eos quoque ac praecipue recidit, qui ipsorum curam habere debent, idest in parentes, tutores, confessarium, institutores et parochum"—can. 860.

[50]"Masses for Children" (paper read by Canon Janssens at the Congress of Priest Adorers in Belgium, May, 1913), *Emmanuel,* XX (1914), 108.

CHAPTER VII

PRECAUTIONS TO BE TAKEN AGAINST ABUSES IN THE FREQUENT RECEPTION OF HOLY COMMUNION

"Whosoever shall eat this bread, or drink the chalice of the Lord unworthily, shall be guilty of the body and blood of the Lord."[1]

It is the nature of men to have little esteem for things to which it is accustomed by frequent use. It is likewise a weakness of man's nature to sometimes heed in larger measure the censure of his fellow beings than the condemnation of his God. These two weaknesses of human nature are especially the causes of the danger of receiving Communion unworthily, and seem to be, as it were, inherent in the widespread practice of frequent and daily Communion. This is especially true when the faithful approach the Holy Sacrament, not singly but in a body, as happens daily in seminaries, religious communities, frequently in colleges and schools for the young, and sometimes even in gatherings which are held for the purpose of receiving the Most Blessed Sacrament at Easter time or on some other solemn occasion. "For it can happen that some one, though conscious of grave sin, may yet approach the Holy Table influenced by the vain fear that if he stays away he will cause astonishment in the others, especially in his superiors, and will be suspected of having committed a grave sin."[2]

Since the time that St. Paul wrote the words quoted at the head of this chapter, the Church has repeatedly insisted upon the necessity of receiving the Holy Eucharist in the state of grace and with the proper intention. But with equal insistence it has encouraged the spread of frequent and daily Communion. Especially since the Council of Trent (1545-1563) it has acted on the truth, so sadly demonstrated between the fifth and sixteenth centuries,

[1] I Cor., XI; 27.

[2] *Reserved Instruction on Daily Communion and Precautions to Be Taken Against Abuses.* S.C. de Sacr., 8 dec. 1938. Private.—Bouscaren, *The Canon Law Digest,* II, 209. The excerpted passages of this Instruction follow the text as supplied by Bouscaren, *ibid.,* pp. 208-215.

and particularly in the heresy of Jansenism,[3] that it is better to accept the responsibility of warring against the dangers inherent in so salutary a practice, than to remove the dangers by discouraging the practice.

Throughout the decrees and laws relative to the promotion of frequent and daily Communion, the reader will note precautionary phrases directed against possible abuses in relation to this great Sacrament. More recently, the Sacred Congregation of the Sacraments issued a reserved instruction on daily Communion and on the precautions to be taken against abuses. The present chapter is concerned with these precautions, and will attempt to present in an orderly way the laws, decrees and official recommendations made in this regard.

Article 1. Regarding Frequent and Daily Communion in General

Canon 863 of the Code of Canon Law contains two phrases which may well be called "precautionary." In legislating that frequent and daily Communion be encouraged among the faithful, the canon qualifies this command by adding "according to the norms handed down in the decrees of the Apostolic See." As has already been seen in the preceding chapter, the decrees make several important definitions concerning the dispositions necessary for the frequent and daily reception of Communion, while urging careful preparation for a more fruitful reception of the Sacrament. These are the norms of which the canon speaks, and in so doing certainly indicates that all encouragement along this line be tempered accordingly. The second precautionary phrase used in the canon introduces the words "rightly disposed" (*rite dispositi*) in expressing the Church's desire, first stated by the Council of Trent (1545-1563),[4] "that at each Mass the faithful who are present should communicate, not only in spiritual desire but also by the sacramental partaking of the Eucharist."

These precautions are enlarged upon, and rules to enforce

[3]*Supra*, pp. 22 ff.

[4]Sess. XXII, *de sacrificio missae*, c. 6.

them are laid down, in the Reserved Instruction of the Sacred Congregation of the Sacraments as issued on December 8, 1938. The first two rules concern the practice of frequent and daily Communion in general, without respect to any particular group or class of people:

> I, 1. "Preachers and spiritual directors, when they either publicly or privately exhort the faithful, particularly young people, to frequent and daily Communion, must not be content with this exhortation, but must at the same time inform them: (a) that daily Communion is not obligatory; (b) that it may not be practiced without the concurrence of the necessary conditions."

The Instruction then offers an official commentary on these two points:

> II, 1, (a) "Frequent and daily Communion is indeed very much recommended, but it is not commanded by any law. It is, therefore, left to each one's devotion and piety. So true is this that even the obligation of Paschal Communion is modified by the clause 'unless by advice of his own priest, for some reasonable cause (the person) judge that he should abstain from it for a time' (c. 859, § 1). Now it follows from this that there is no occasion for astonishment or suspicion if, where the practice of daily Communion is in use, someone occasionally abstains. And if this truth is clearly grasped, the vain fear which can be the occasion of receiving Communion unworthily will be entirely removed. (b) Holy Communion, which is *life to the good,* is *death to the wicked.* Hence, first of all, the *state of grace* is required. Horror of sacrilege must be thoroughly inculcated, and attention must be directed to the law according to which 'no one who is conscious of mortal sin, however persuaded he be that he is also contrite, shall go to Communion without previously making a sacramental confession . . .' (c. 856).
>
> "There is further required a *right* or pious *intention,* which 'consists in this, that a person approach the Holy Table, not from routine, or vanity, or human motives, but because he wishes to please God, to be more closely united to Him in charity, and to come with his infirmities and defects to that divine physician' (Decree, *Sacra Tridentina Synodus,* n. 2).
>
> "Moreover, 'in order that frequent and daily Communion may be received with greater prudence and be crowned with

greater merit, it is necessary that the advice of the confessor be obtained' (Decree cited, n. 5)."[5]

There are two other recommendations found in the Instruction which, while they are applied to specific groups of individuals, nevertheless have application to frequent and daily Communion in general. The first of these recommendations is found in article n. 2 of the Instruction:

> "Together with frequent Communion, frequent confession also must be promoted: not that confession must precede every Communion, unless a person is conscious of mortal sin, but that the faithful who live in communities should not only go to confession on stated days, but should be free to go, without any remarks from their Superiors, to a confessor of their choice, and, what is especially important, that they should have the opportunity to make a confession also shortly before the time of Communion."

While this regulation is primarily intended for "the faithful who live in communities," and cannot be urged strictly for those outside of communities, it must be conceded that the promotion of frequent confession among all frequent communicants is a laudable and worthwhile practice. For while the danger of a person's act of sacrilegious reception out of human respect is magnified by the circumstances of community life, it is nevertheless present to some degree in parish life, when friends and neighbors are accustomed to receive Holy Communion daily at the same altar rail.

There is no law which demands that the faithful be given easy access to confession before or during every Mass at which Holy Communion is to be distributed, except that stated in canon 467: "The pastor must . . . administer the Sacraments to the faithful, as often as they lawfully petition (him) . . ." The right of the

[5]The translation furnished by Father Bouscaren in *The Canon Law Digest*, II, 210, seems a little strong on one point. The original latin text reads: "*Ut frequens et quotidiana Communio maiori prudentia fiat uberiorique merito augeatur, oportet ut Confessarii consilium intercedat.*" *Oportet*, while indicating a high recommendation, hardly has the same force as *necesse est, opus est*, or even *debet*. It may further be pointed out that this *necessity* of consulting a confessor, even if it be admitted, does not apply to the licit and useful reception of the Holy Eucharist, but rather to a more prudent and more meritorious reception. Cf. *supra*, p. 152.

faithful to petition is clearly stated in canon 682: "The laity has a right to receive from the clergy, according to the norm of ecclesiastical discipline, spiritual benefits and especially those aids which are necessary for salvation."

This much, at least, can be deduced from the aforementioned canons: 1) that no pastor could lawfully refuse to hear the confession of a frequent or daily communicant whenever he is asked, unless, from past experience, he knows that in a particular case the petition is an abuse of the law, and 2) that the right of the laity to make a petition implies an obligation on the part of the pastor to be reasonably available. Hence it would certainly be an abuse if it were practically impossible for a person to go to confession except on Saturday afternoons and evenings. In parishes, therefore, where the laudable practice of providing a confessor before or during every Mass at which Holy Communion is to be distributed is not practicable, it seems incumbent on the pastor to make it known publicly that he will hear the confession of anyone asking him to do so at any reasonable time.[6]

[6]A decree of Pope Pius X, dated February 14, 1906, and issued through the Sacred Congregation of Indulgences, and now embodied in canon 931, § 3, of the Code of Canon Law, definitely relieved daily communicants of the obligation of confessing within any specified interval of time in order to qualify themselves for the gaining of indulgences. The decree granted to all the faithful who, while in a state of grace and having a right and devout intention, are accustomed daily to receive the Holy Sacrament of the Altar, even if they once or twice in a week omit their daily Communion, the right to avail themselves of the Idult of Clement XIII (1758-1769) (cf. *Fontes*, n. 4993), so that without the fulfillment of the condition of weekly confession, which in other circumstances was still of obligation in this matter, they could gain the various indulgences falling due during the course of the week.

The Indult of Pope Clement XIII had granted to all the faithful "who in striving to purify their souls by means of the frequent confession of their sins were accustomed, unless they were legitimately hindered, to approach the Sacrament of Penance at least once a week, and were not conscious of having committed any mortal sin since their latest confession, the privilege of gaining all indulgences whatsoever, without the actual confession which otherwise would have been necessary for gaining them: . . . *Decreta Authentica S.C. Indulgentiis Sacrisque Reliquis Praepositae ab anno 1668 ad annum 1882,* edita iussu et auctoritate SS. D.N. Leonis PP. XIII, (6 vols. in 7, New York and Cincinnati, 1883), n. 231.

It is quite evident from the foregoing regulations regarding the requirements for the gaining of indulgences that there existed no law demanding a weekly or even monthly confession for the daily communicant who steadfastly avoided all serious sin if he was to qualify himself for the gaining of the ordi-

The second recommendation made for communities but applicable to frequent and daily Communion in general is to be found in the Instruction under II, n. 3, *b*:

> "In communities of boys and girls there should never be an announcement of a *general Communion* with special solemnity, and even outside communities, the very name 'general Communion' should either not be used at all or its meaning carefully explained: namely, that all are invited to the Holy Table, but no one is obliged to approach, on the contrary each individual is entirely free to abstain from it."[7]

The Instruction is here of course speaking primarily of young people in communities, but by its own words, "even outside communities," it extends the application of this passage to the faithful in general. The Instruction does not seem hereby to forbid the custom of the various parochial societies of adult persons in accordance with which their members receive Holy Communion in a body on certain Sundays of the month. Rather, any conveyance of the idea that each member is obliged to receive, or the impression that one who does not receive is worthy of criticism, is strictly to be avoided. Hence, in announcing Communion Sunday for the various societies, the pastor should make special efforts to emphasize the complete freedom of the individual's conscience, and that it is perfectly normal for some people to abstain from receiving Holy Communion for reasons other than the lack of the state of grace.

Article 2. Regarding Religious Communities

> II, 2, c) "As regards all religious communities of men or women, the provisions of law are found in canon 518 and the following canons, and they are to be religiously observed in their letter and spirit. 'In each house of a clerical institute,

nary indulgences. If confession, weekly or even monthly, was not required as a condition for the gaining of indulgences on the part of daily communicants precisely for the reason that their daily reception of Holy Communion supplanted the need of meeting the condition of weekly confession, then it is also deducible that weekly or even monthly confession was not a condition for the daily reception of Holy Communion. The advisability of the practice of frequent confession for daily communicants is quite clearly demonstrated in the Instruction of 1938, but it is impossible to show that it is demanded by any law.

[7]Bouscaren, *The Canon Law Digest*, II, 213.

several duly approved confessors in proportion to the number of members, must be deputed, with the faculty, in the case of an exempt institute, to absolve also from cases which are reserved in the institute' (c. 518, § 1). 'Superiors must be careful that they do not, either in person or through another, by force, fear, or importunate persuasion, nor by any other means, induce any of their subjects to go to confession to themselves' (c. 518, § 3). '. . . If a religious, even exempt, for his peace of conscience goes to a confessor who is approved by the Ordinary of the place, even though he is not among those designated, the confession is valid and licit, every privilege to the contrary being hereby revoked; and the confessor can absolve the religious also from sins and censures which are reserved in the institute' (c. 519). 'Every community of women religious should be given an extraordinary confessor, who should go to the religious house at least four times a year, and to whom all the religious must present themselves, at least to receive his blessing' (c. 521, § 1). 'Ordinaries of places in which there are communities of women religious must designate a number of (*aliquot*) priests for each house, to whom the sisters can easily go in particular cases, without the necessity of applying to the Ordinary each time' (c. 521, § 2). 'If any woman religious, for her peace of conscience and greater progress in the way of God, asks for any special confessor or spiritual director, the Ordinary should easily grant the request . . .' (c. 520, § 2). 'So too if any woman religious asks for one of . . . the confessors (designated by the Ordinaries of places for each house of women religious), no Superioress may, in person or through others, directly or indirectly, ask the reason of the request, nor refuse it by word or act, nor in any way show that she takes it ill' (c. 521, § 3). Moreover, notwithstanding the above provisions, 'if . . . any woman religious, for her peace of conscience, goes to a confessor who is approved for women by the Ordinary of the place, the confession made in any church or oratory even semi-public or in any other place lawfully destined for the confessions of women (Commission for the Interpretation of the Code, 24 Nov., 1920 [AAS, XII (1920), 575] is valid and licit, every privilege to the contrary being hereby revoked; nor may the Superioress forbid it or inquire about it even indirectly; and the women religious are not bound to give any account to the Superioress' (c. 522). Likewise: 'all women religious, when they are seriously ill, although there be no danger of death, may send for any priest who is approved to hear the confessions of women,

> even though he is not designated for religious, and may as often as they choose, as long as the serious illness continues, make their confession to him, nor may the Superioress forbid it either directly or indirectly' (c. 523).
>
> "Nuns who are bound by the law of enclosure and who are not allowed to go out or to go to their own church or to a semipublic oratory, have the same faculty: they may call any confessor they choose who is approved for the confessions of women to come to the ordinary confessional of the monastery to hear their confessions (cf. Reply of the aforesaid Commission of Interpretation, of 28 Dec., 1927),[8] and, if they are seriously ill, even to their own room, with the necessary precautions, nor may the Superioress forbid it directly or indirectly."[9]

After presenting this summary of law regarding the freedom with which all religious must be provided for a ready approach to the Sacrament of Penance, the Instruction makes several recommendations for the enforcement of these laws:

> "Ecclesiastics, therefore, who are delegated for communities of women religious should do all in their power to prevent Superioresses from inquiring even indirectly why their religious subjects sent for or went to another confessor; and they should inform the said Superioresses that they have no power to forbid this to their subjects in any way. The aforesaid delegates must know that it can easily happen that women religious fear to ask the Superioress for an extraordinary confessor, and so are not free to provide for the welfare of their conscience. Let them therefore carefully watch that in a matter of such importance the liberty which has been wisely provided by law for women religious be not diminished."

The "ecclesiastics . . . delegated for communities of women religious," here spoken of, evidently are not the ordinary and extraordinary confessors appointed for the purpose of hearing the confessions of these religious. Canon 524, § 3, strictly forbids the ordinary and extraordinary confessor from interfering, in any way,

[8] *AAS,* XX (1928), 61; Bouscaren, *The Canon Law Digest,* I, 296.

[9] Bouscaren, *The Canon Law Digest,* II, 211-212. A full treatment of the various questions related to the confessors of religious, the right of women religious to summon a confessor of their choice or to take advantage of the presence of a priest for confession, etc., is to be found in the work of McCormick, *Confessors of Religious,* The Catholic University of America Canon Law Studies, n. 33 (Washington, D.C.: The Catholic University of America, 1926).

in the internal or external rule of the community.[10] Furthermore, any ecclesiastic having power in the external forum over the aforesaid women religious is thereby disqualified for appointment as confessor to the same women religious.[11] Hence, one must conclude that the ecclesiastics spoken of are those delegated with some power in the external forum over the women religious, such as the Vicar General for Religious and those appointed for the quinquennial visitation of religious houses according to the norms of canons 512 and 513.[12] It will therefore be incumbent upon these delegates of the bishop, or upon the bishop himself, to guard against any abuse of the freedom provided by the law for women religious.

[10]Confessarii religiosarum tum ordinarii tum extraordinarii interno vel externo communitatis regimini nullo modo sese immisceant.—can. 524, § 3.

[11]In munus confessarii religiosarum et ordinarii et extraordinarii deputentur sacerdotes . . . nullam potestatem in easdem religiosas in foro externo habentes —can. 524, § 1.

[12]Can. 618.—§ 2. In religionibus tamen iuris pontificii Ordinario loci non licet:

2°. Sese ingerere in regimen internum ac disciplinam, exceptis casibus in iure expressis; nihilominus in religionibus laicalibus ipse potest ac debet inquirere num disciplina ad constitutionum normam vigeat, num quid sana doctrina morumve probitas detrimenti ceperit, num contra clausuram peccatum sit, num Sacramenta aequa stataque frequentia suscipiantur; et, si Superiores de gravibus forte abusibus admoniti opportune non providerint, ipse per se consulat; si qua tamen maioris momenti occurrant, quae moram non patiantur, decernat statim; decretum vero ad Sanctam Sedem deferat.

Can. 512.—§ 1. Ordinarius loci per se vel per alium quinto quoque anno visitare debet:

1°. Singula monialium monasteria quae sibi vel Sedi Apostolicae immediate subiecta sunt;

2°. Singulas domos sive virorum sive mulierum Congregationis iuris dioecesani.

§ 2. Visitare quoque eodem tempore debet:

1°. Monasteria monialium, quae regularibus subduntur, . . . circa alia omnia, si Superior regularis ea a quinque annis non visitaverit; . . .

3°. Singulas domos Congregationis laicalis pontificii non solum in iis, de quibus in superiore numero, sed etiam in aliis, quae ad internam disciplinam spectant, ad normam tamen can. 618, § 2, n. 2. . . .

Can. 513.—Visitator ius et officium habet interrogandi religiosos quos oportere iudicaverit et cognoscendi de iis quae ad visitationem spectant; omnes autem religiosi obligatione tenentur respondendi secundum veritatem, nec Superioribus fas est quoquo modo eos ab hac obligatione avertere aut visitationis scopum aliter impedire.

The Instruction is careful, however, to note the provision of canon 520, § 2:

> "Of course, the exercise of this liberty of conscience must be appropriately combined in each community with the regular observance of discipline, which the Ordinaries of places should try to preserve intact; and they should likewise take care that no abuses arise from the use of these privileges, and that such as may have already crept in be cautiously and prudently removed, always without prejudice to liberty of conscience."[13]

The Instruction also calls attention to the provision of canon 528, which calls for the appointment of an ordinary and extraordinary confessor for lay institutes of men.[14]

A final observation may be made regarding religious communities by recalling some remarks of the Instruction regarding frequent and daily Communion in general.

II, 2, of the Instruction reads in part as follows:

> "Together with frequent Communion, frequent confession also must be promoted: . . . the faithful who live in communities . . . should have the opportunity to make a confession also shortly before the time of Communion. a) Accordingly Pastors of souls must make every effort to provide in each community, according to the number of the members, one or two confessors to whom each one may freely go. They must keep in mind the rule that, where frequent and daily Communion is in vogue, frequent and daily opportunity for sacramental confession, as far as that is possible, must also be afforded. It is desirable also that other confessors, chosen from among those that are approved, be given rather frequently to all communities."[15]

Article 3. Regarding Seminaries

II, 2, *b*) "As regards seminaries we have the provisions of canons 1358, 1361, and 1367 of the Code of Canon Law, according to which there must be in every seminary at least

[13]Bouscaren, *The Canon Law Digest*, II, 213.

[14]Etiam in laicalibus virorum religionibus deputetur, ad normam can. 874, §. 1, 875, § 2, confessarius ordinarius et extraordinarius; et si religiosus aliquem specialem confessarium expostulet, illum Superior concedat, nullo modo petitionis rationem inquirens neque id aegre se ferre demonstrans—can. 528.

[15]Bouscaren, *The Canon Law Digest*, II, 210.

two ordinary confessors and a spiritual director,[16] and besides the ordinary confessors others must be designated to whom the students have free access:[17] if these confessors live outside the seminary and a student asks that any of them be called, the rector must send for him, without in any way asking the reason for the request or showing that he takes it ill: if they live in the seminary, the student must be allowed freely to go to him, without prejudice to the discipline of the seminary.[18] Let Superiors consider the serious opinion of Saint Alphonsus, namely that students of a seminary are in great danger of committing sacrileges if they always confess to confessors who are known to them. (Cf. S. Alphonsus, *Regolamento per i Seminari,* § 1, n. 3.) Bishops should see to it that the students go to confession at least once a week."[19]

Beside these prescriptions of the Code of Canon Law, the general provisions of the Instruction mentioned above in regard to frequent and daily Communion in general and in regard to religious communities are to be applied to seminaries. Furthermore, in junior seminaries, the provisions of the following article dealing with children and young people should be carefully studied and judiciously applied.

The Instruction, in order to remove any possible semblance of coercion or undue pressure on the seminarian to receive the Holy Eucharist in opposition to the dictates of his conscience, forbade superiors of seminaries and other institutions of the kind to make the frequency of the reception of Holy Communion a point in the judgment made concerning the subject's progress in piety:

II, 3, *a*) "In seminaries and other institutions of the kind, where at stated times a judgment on each student is made by

[16]Curandum ut in quolibet Seminario adsint . . . duo saltem confessarii ordinarii et director spiritus—can. 1358.

[17]Praeter confessarios ordinarios, alii confesarii designentur ad quos libere alumni accedere possint—can. 1361, § 1.

[18]Si ii confessarii extra Seminarium degant, et alumnus aliquem eorum acciri postulet, illum rector arcessat, nullo modo petitionis rationem inquirens neque se aegre id ferre demonstrans; si in Seminario habitent, ipso alumnus libere adire potest, salva Seminarii disciplina—can. 1361, § 2.

[19]Curent Episcopi ut alumni Seminarii: . . . Semel saltem in hebdomada ad sacramentum poenitentiae accedant . . . —can. 1367, 2°. Cf. Bouscaren, *The Canon Law Digest,* II, 210-211.

> Superiors as regards piety, study and discipline, the said Superiors, in giving their judgment regarding the progress of the young man in piety, must take no account of this greater or less assiduity in receiving the Most Blessed Eucharist."[20]

An earlier Instruction of the Sacred Congregation of the Sacraments, dated December 27, 1930, addressed to the Most Reverend Ordinaries, and entitled: "On the testing of candidates before they are promoted to orders," included a form for the investigation to be made through the pastors of the candidates. Question 2 of this form asks whether he (the candidate) goes to confession and receives Holy Communion often and devoutly.[21]

While one can reconcile this question with the prohibition of the Instruction of the same Congregation issued in 1938 by noting that each applies to a different investigation and to a different set of circumstances, the earlier stipulation seems to be out of keeping with the spirit of the later Instruction. For, if "greater or less assiduity in receiving the Most Blessed Eucharist" is not to be taken into account by Superiors in judging the progress of a young man in piety for the reason that he may thereby be impelled to receive sacrilegiously, the same ought to apply in judging a young man's fitness for the reception of orders. It seems, therefore, that the question relating to the frequency of the reception of Holy Communion on the part of seminarians as found in the questionnaire for the investigation to be made by pastors should be stricken out. For it must be emphasized that, while the frequent and daily reception of Holy Communion is a most laudable and salutary practice, it is by no means obligatory; nor is it certain proof of one's greater or less piety.

The Instruction further stresses this point in saying:

> "The Superior [and, by implication, all who are liable to engender reverential fear] should say very plainly to his subjects that he is in general much pleased with their frequent approach to the Holy Table, but that he has no word of reproach for those who do not receive, but rather sees in this a sign of liberty and of a tender and delicate conscience. And

[20]Bouscaren, *The Canon Law Digest,* II, 213.

[21]Bouscaren, *The Canon Law Digest,* I, 472.

let him not contradict this declaration by his conduct, nor give any indication that he seems to notice those who go to Communion frequently, and to praise them while blaming the others."[22]

ARTICLE 4. REGARDING CHILDREN AND YOUNG PEOPLE

The special solicitude of the Holy See for children and young people has been amply demonstrated throughout this work. This solicitude on the part of the Holy See, coupled with the fact that the young are the reserve of the Church, and that they have more immediate need of Communion, as Father Jules Lintelo remarks, either for preserving holy purity or for regaining it,[23] should leave little room for hesitancy on the part of any priest to encourage frequent and daily Communion among the young. However, just as there is special need of Holy Communion among the young, so there are special problems to be encountered in the promoting of the frequent reception of It. Children are particularly susceptible to reverential fear; their realization of sin and sacrilege is limited; their tendency toward conformity and obedience is undoubtedly greater than their judgment of comparative values. Hence there is far greater danger among the young than among adults of approaching the altar rail unworthily or for unworthy motives.

The Instruction of 1938 has singled out for correction a number of common practices which tend toward the regimentation of the young in their reception of Holy Communion, thus depriving them of a complete liberty of conscience. The Instruction also makes some recommendations intended to guarantee the preservation of this essential freedom.

As is emphasized throughout the Instruction, the provision of confessors is perhaps the greatest safeguard against unworthy Communions. Over and above the general directives that frequent confession be encouraged and that adequate confessors be supplied frequently and especially a short time before the time of Communion, the Instruction orders that:

[22]Bouscaren, *The Canon Law Digest,* II, 213.

[23]Lintelo, *The Eucharistic Triduum, an aid to priests in preaching frequent and daily Communion according to the Decrees of H.H. Pius X,* translated from the French (2. ed.) by F. M. de Zuluette, S.J. (Westmonasterii, 1909), 97.

". . . in all communities of young people of either sex, every effort must be made that a confessor be at hand and easily accessible at the time when Communion is being distributed to the community."[24]

Obviously, it is the desire of the Sacred Congregation that, in places where enough priests are available, at least one should go to the confessional before and during the Mass which the young members of the school, college, or any other institution, are accustomed to attend. Whenever this is impossible, it seems incumbent on the priest who celebrates the Mass to go to the confessional a short time before the time of Mass, in order that those who have need may confess without the embarrassment of personally requesting the priest to hear his or her confession.

Such great danger of unworthy Communion among the young lies in the practice of regimentation that the Sacred Congregation has strictly forbidden two practices which have been common enough in many of our schools and institutions. The first has already been mentioned in regard to frequent and daily Communion in general; namely, that "in communities of boys and girls there should never be an announcement of a *general Communion* with special solemnity . . ." The reason for this prohibition is clear enough. It creates a situation wherein a young person may be forced to choose between an unworthy Communion and what he feels to be the public acknowledgment of his guilt. Even when ample opportunity for confession is afforded, this situation is not entirely prevented, for it may happen that the necessary dispositions for sacramental absolution are not present. Hence, the Sacred Congregation's strict ruling.

This does not, however, rule out the prudent encouraging of the reception of Holy Communion on feasts of special solemnity and the like. It is laudable, according to decrees cited above, to stir up in the hearts of the young a desire to receive Communion; indeed, it is of obligation to do so. But in so doing, the director must sedulously avoid using such expressions as "the entire school (or class) will receive Communion," or "all members of the Rosary

[24]II, 2, *d*) of the Instruction—Bouscaren, *The Canon Law Digest*, II, 213.

Society are to receive," or any other phrase which might be interpreted by the young person to mean that a one-hundred-per-cent attendance is expected or required. Even in those societies of the young which are particularly dedicated to the fostering of devotion to the Blessed Sacrament this precaution must be taken.

The second practice forbidden by the Instruction is the one which so often is "justified" in the name of preserving order. It is customary in many schools, institutions and even parishes at the children's Mass, to have the children march in ranks to the Communion rail. The Sacred Congregation has considered this to be a source of danger, and has therefore forbidden it in these words:

> "When Holy Communion is being received all those things are to be avoided which create greater difficulty for a young person who wishes to abstain from Holy Communion, but in such a way that his abstinence will not be noticed; hence there should be no express invitation, no rigid and quasi-military order in coming up, no insignia to be worn by those who receive Communion, etc."[25]

Again the Instruction is quite clear in its meaning. The order which would be preserved by the segregation of those who express their intention to receive, or the approach to the altar rail one by one or by the pew number in which one is stationed for Mass, is to be sacrificed for the greater good of preserving complete freedom of conscience in those who may wish to abstain unnoticed. Children should be taught the ordinary signal for Communion time and be permitted to approach the altar with complete freedom.

And what is said here of young people in institutions applies equally to gatherings of the young for parochial functions. The Instruction is explicit:

> "Promoters and directors of gatherings of young people which are convened, for example in public schools, for the sake of receiving Holy Communion, must take notice that in such gatherings there are dangers akin to those which exist in communities, and they must employ all the means for removing them, not only by announcing that each one is free to receive Communion or not, and by supplying sufficient opportunity for confession, but also by striving to remove all circum-

[25] II, 3, *c*) of the Instruction—Bouscaren, *The Canon Law Digest,* II, 214.

stances which might expose those who do not receive to astonishment from the others, as was said above."[26]

Hence, Junior Holy Name Societies, and those Holy Name Societies which admit young members, Sodalities, Leagues and other gatherings of young people, are to be considered, in this matter, the same as though they were communities. They may be permitted to attend Mass in a body on special days, and to wear the insignia of their society, but never in such a way that particular attention will be focused upon those members who do not receive Holy Communion. Hence, there should again be no quasi-military order in the approach to the altar rail, and no enforced segregation from the rest of the congregation, no mandatory wearing of the insignia.

Finally, what has been said of Superiors of communities in the matter of encouraging frequent and daily Communion applies also to all who possess authority of any kind over the young.

> "The Superior should say very plainly to his subjects that he is in general much pleased with their frequent approach to the Holy Table, but that he has no word of reproach for those who do not receive, but rather sees in this a sign of liberty and of a tender and delicate conscience. And let him not contradict this declaration by his conduct, nor give any indication that he seems to notice those who go to Communion frequently, and to praise them while blaming others."[27]

Article 5. Regarding the Sick

In general, Communion for the sick who are confined to their beds at home or in hospitals does not present the problems discussed above. According to the *Roman Ritual*[28] the priest who brings Holy Communion to the sick person is always to ask whether he wishes to go to confession and whether he is well disposed for receiving the Most Blessed Sacrament. This, of course, is to be done privately and in such a way that no extraordinary embarrassment would be caused. If this presciption is always carried out, most of the danger of a sacrilegious reception of Holy Communion among the sick will be removed.

[26] II, 3, *e*) of the Instruction—Bouscaren, *The Canon Law Digest,* II, 214.
[27] II, 3, *a*) of the Instruction—Bouscaren, *The Canon Law Digest,* II, 213.
[28] Titulus IV, caput IV, *De communione infirmorum,* n. 16.

However, in communities and hospitals where it is customary to omit this part of the rubrics in the several rooms to be visited after one has fulfilled them in the room of the first visit,[29] the danger of someone's receiving Holy Communion unworthily because of embarrassment or confusion again becomes present. Hence, the Instruction of 1938 made it a point to note that:

> "The Superior of the community should see to it that Holy Communion be not brought to the sick who do not expressly ask for it."[30]

It would undoubtedly be the safest practice to conform to the opinion of O'Kane,[31] who wrote: "As a general rule, the Blessed Sacrament is not to be brought to the sick person until he has been previously visited by the priest, and has made his confession, because he might not be in a condition to receive Communion, or even to be absolved, on the first visit of the priest." This rule could probably be relaxed to some extent, for example, in the case of a sick person who has been a daily communicant over a long period of time. But when dealing with comparatively strange patients in a hospital, it should not be assumed that a request for Holy Communion on one day indicates a desire to receive daily.

In view of the embarrassment likely to be caused to a person in consequence of his refusal to arrange for the reception of Holy Communion when asked by a nurse or Sister, it seems most proper that the chaplain, on his daily visit to the sick, personally determine who will receive Holy Communion on the following day.

[29]This practice was sanctioned by the Sacred Congregation of Rites in an Instruction given on January 9, 1929.—*AAS*, XXI (1929), 43.

[30]II, 3, *d*) of the Instruction—Bouscaren, *The Canon Law Digest*, II, 214.

[31]*Notes on the Rubrics of the Roman Ritual* (new edition completely revised in accordance with the latest [1925] *editio typica* of the *Rituale Romanum*, and Decrees of the Sacred Congregations by the Rev. Michael J. Fallon, D.C.L. Dean, St. Patrick's College, Maynooth. Dublin: James Duffy and Co., Limited, 1938), p. 420.

CONCLUSIONS

The following conclusions may be derived from the foregoing study.

1) The practice of frequent Holy Communion was introduced in the very early years of Christianity, subsided with the rapid growth of the Church after the fifth century, began slowly to revive after the Council of Trent (1545-1563), and received its culminating impetus from Pope Pius X in 1906 with the issuance of the Decree *Sacra Tridentina Synodus.*

2) The practice of frequent or daily Holy Communion was never, and is not now, obligatory for any person regardless of his state in life.

3) The Church has consistently urged the faithful to practice frequent and daily Communion, though at times her voice was unheard among the disputes of theologians and the general indifference of the faithful.

4) It is to be considered the *optandum* of the Church that all the faithful, if they be not otherwise excluded by law, receive Holy Communion each time they assist at the Holy Sacrifice of the Mass.

5) Within the respective sphere of their authority and supervision, parish priests, confessors, preachers, superiors of religious and other Catholic institutions, teachers and parents are seriously obliged to promote the practice of frequent and daily Holy Communion among all the faithful.

6) The Holy See has of late years extended generous privileges to foster frequent and daily Communion among those of the faithful who might otherwise be impeded.

7) Serious thought and action must be taken for the sake of forestalling the abuses peculiar to the practice of frequent and daily Communion.

8) The Apostolic Indult of 1946, granted to the Most Reverend Ordinaries of the United States to be exercised in favor of

the sick who are hospitalized, may be applied lawfully to the following classes of patients, provided that they be actually in a place which is habitually set aside for the therapeutic care of the sick, injured or infirm:

a. all who are suffering from any pathological condition in any stage of development;

b. expectant and recent mothers, even though no true sickness be evident;

c. convalescents from disease or bodily injury;

d. sufferers from diseases of the mind, provided that they are otherwise capable of receiving Holy Communion;

e. anyone who, in the common estimation of prudent men, can be said to be in a state of ill health.

9) The two conditions, of sickness namely and of hospitalization, constitute of themselves the just and reasonable cause for the granting of a dispensation as demanded by canon 84. Hence, no further cause, such as the necessity of taking medicine, or the presence of a grave inconvenience in the keeping of the fast, is required.

10) The Apostolic Indult of 1946, granted to the Most Reverend Ordinaries of the United States to be exercised in favor of all those who habitually work after midnight, may be utilized lawfully for:

a. those who work at least five nights out of the week;

b. those who work five nights out of every second or third week, but only for those weeks during which they so work.

11) A night worker so dispensed need not apply for a new dispensation after an interruption of several weeks in consequence of a temporary lay-off or work stoppage.

12) A dispensed night-worker may lawfully use his dispensation on Sundays, on feasts of precept, and on one other day of the week, regardless of whether or not the day on which he uses it be preceded by work after midnight.

13) Nursing Sisters must qualify as habitual night workers in the same way as the other workers in order to become dispensed from the strict Eucharistic fast for the daily reception of Holy Communion. However, in their case, night work on two or three nights of the week suffices to qualify them as habitual night workers.

14) Wherever frequent or daily Communion is practiced, adequate opportunity for sacramental confession must be provided frequently, i.e. at least two or three times a week.

15) Great care must be exercised in order that everyone be provided the opportunity of abstaining, relatively unnoticed, from the reception of Holy Communion if he should so desire. This is particularly applicable to all those who live in communities and to the young.

16) The practice of "general Communions" for groups and societies, especially of the young, should be judiciously supplanted with other means of encouraging the frequent reception of Holy Communion.

BIBLIOGRAPHY

Sources

Acta Apostolicae Sedis, Commentarium Officiale, Romae, 1909—.

Acta Sanctae Sedis, 41 vols., Romae, 1865-1908.

Bouscaren, T. Lincoln, *The Canon Law Digest,* 2 vols., Milwaukee, The Bruce Publishing Company, 1934-1943.

Bruns, H. T., *Canones Apostolorum et Conciliorum Saeculorum IV-VII,* 2 vols., Berolini, 1839.

Bullarum Diplomatum et Privilegiorum Sanctorum Romanorum Pontificum Tauriensis Editio, 25 vols., 24 vols. et Appendix, Augustae Taurinorum, 1857-1872.

Caeremoniale Episcoporum, Romae, Pustet, 1886.

Capitularia Regum Francorum, 2 vols., ed. Stephanus Balusius, Parisiis, 1677 (Reimpressio ex Typis Francisci-Augustini, 1780).

Catechism of the Council of Trent, The, Published by command of Pope Pius V, translated into English by the Rev. J. Donovan, New York, The Catholic Publication Society, 1829.

Catechismus ex decreto Concilii Tridentini ad Parochos, Pii V Pontificis Max. et deinde Clementis XIII iussu editus, Editio stereotypa, Romae, Marietti, 1930.

Codex Iuris Canonici Pii X Pontificis Maximi iussu digestus Benedicti Papae XV auctoritate promulgatus, Romae, Typis Polygottis Vaticanis, 1917 (Reimpressio 1934).

Codicis Iuris Canonici Fontes, cura Emi Petri Card. Gasparri editi, 9 vols., Romae (postea Civitate Vaticana), Typis Polyglottis Vaticanis, 1923-1939. (Vols. VII-IX ed. cura et studio Emi Iustiniani Card. Seredi.)

Collectanea S. Congregationis de Propaganda Fide, 2 vols., Romae, Typographia S.C. de Propaganda Fide, 1907.

Corpus Iuris Canonici, Editio Lipsiensis II post Aemilii Ludovici Richteri curas instruxit Aemilius Friedberg, 1879-1881. Editio anastatice repetita, Lipsiae, Ex Officina Bernhardi Tauchnitz, 1922.

Corpus Scriptorum Ecclesiasticorum Latinorum, ed. consilio et impensis Academiae Litterarum Caesariae Vindobonensis, Vindobonae, 1866—.

Decreta Authentica S.C. Indulgentiis Sacrisque Reliquiis Praepositae ab anno 1668 ad annum 1882, edita iussu et auctoritate SS. D.N. Leonis PP. XIII, 6 vols. in 7, New York and Cincinnati, 1883.

Decreta Authentica Congregationis Sacrorum Rituum, 6 vols., Romae, Typis Polyglottis Vaticanis, 1898-1927.

Decretum Gratiani Emendatum et Notationibus illustratum una cum Glossis, Romae, 1582.

Denzinger, Henricus, *Enchiridion Symbolorum Definitionum, et Declarationum De* Rebus Fidei et Morum, quod a Cl. Bannwart denuo compositum, iteratis curis ed. Ioannes Bapt. Umberg, 21-23 ed., Friburgi Brisgoviae, Herder and Co., 1937.

Didascalia et Constitutiones Apostolorum, ed. Franciscus X. Funk, 2 vols., Paderbornae, 1905.

Die griechischen christlichen Schriftsteller der ersten drei Jahrhunderte—herausg. von der Kirchenväter—Kommission der konigl. preussischen Akademie der Wissenchaften, Leipzig, 1897—.

Facultates Castrenses, editio altera, commentario aucta, New York, 1942.

Florilegium Patristicum tam veteris quam medii aevi auctores complectens, ed. Bernhardus Geyer et Johannes Zellinger: 50 fasciculi, Bonnae: Sumptibus Petri Hanstein, 1911-1940; Fasciculus VII, *Monumenta eucharistica et liturgica vetustissima,* collegit notis et prolegomenis instruxit Johannes Quasten.

Hefele, C.-LeClercq, H., *Histoire des Conciles,* 10 vols. in 19, Paris, 1907-1938.

Jaffe, Philippus, *Regesta Pontificum Romanorum ad annum 1198,* 2 ed., curantibus G. Wattenbach, F. Kaltenbrunner, P. Ewald, S. Lowenfeld, 2 vols. in 1, Lipsiae, 1885-1888.

Leonis XIII Pontificis Maximi Acta, 23 vols., Romae, 1881-1905.

Lexicon Totius Latinitatis, Aegidii Forcellini Seminarii Patavini Alumni cura et studio Lucubratum; deinde Josephi Furlanetto opera auctum et emendatum; tandem Francisco Corradini (Toms. I, II, III) et Josepho Perin (Tom. IV) ejusdem seminarii alumnis curantibus auctius emendatus melioremque in formam redactam, 19 vols., Patavii, Typis Seminariis, 1920.

Mansi, Ioannes, *Sacrorum Conciliorum Nova et Amplissima Collectio,* 53 vols. in 60, Parisiis-Arnham-Leipzig, 1901-1927.

Monumenta Germaniae Historica, Legum Sectio III, Concilia, Tomus II (*Concilia Aevi Karolini*), Pars I, ed. Albertus Werminghoff, Hannoverae, Lipsiae, 1904.

———— Epistolae Selectae, Tom. II, Fasc. I, ed. E. Caspar, Berolini, 1920.

Murray's (A. H.) *New English Dictionary on Historical Principles,* Oxford, The Clarendon Press, 1901.

Normae secundum quas S. Cong. Ep. et Reg. procedere solet in approbandis Novis Institutis Votorum simplicium, Romae, Typis S. Cong. de Propaganda Fide, 1901.

Pii IX Pontificis Maximi Acta, 9 vols., Romae, 1856-1878.

Rituale Romanum Pauli V Pontificis Maximi iussu editum, a Benedicto XIV et a Pio X castigatum et auctum, Romae, 1903.

Schroeder, H. J., *Canons and Decrees of the Council of Trent, Original Text with English Translation,* St. Louis, Herder, 1941.

Thesaurus Graecae Linguae, ab H. Stephano constructus, 7 vols., ed. nova auctior et emendatior, London, Valpianis, 1822.

Webster's International Dictionary, 2 ed., unabridged, Springfield, Mass., Merriam Co., 1944.

REFERENCE WORKS

Anglin, Thomas F., *The Eucharistic Fast,* The Catholic University of America Canon Law Studies, n. 124, Washington, D.C., The Catholic University of America Press, 1941.

Arnauld, Antoine, *De la Frequente Communion,* 11. ed., Lyons, 1739.

Arregui, Antonius M., *Summarium Theologiae Moralis,* 13. ed. reprint, Westminster, Md., The Newman Bookshop, 1944.

Augustine, Charles, *A Commentary on the New Code of Canon Law,* 8 vols.; vol. IV, *On the Sacraments (except Matrimony) and Sacramentals,* 2. ed., St. Louis, B. Herder Book Co., 1921.

Ballerini Antonius, *Opus Theologicum Morale in Busenbaum Medullam,* 7 vols., Prati, 1889-1893.

Benedictus XIV, *De Synodo Dioecesana,* 2 vols., Parmae, 1764.

Boich, Henricus, *Commentaria in Quinque Decretalium libros,* Venetiis, 1576.

Bonaventure, St., *Opera Omnia,* 10 vols., Quaracchi, 1882-1902.

Cappello, Felix M., *Tractatus Canonico-Moralis de Sacramentis,* 3 vols. in 6, Romae, Marietti, 1932-1939. Vol. I, *De Eucharistia,* 3. ed., 1938.

Cicognani, Amleto G., *Canon Law,* 2. revised edition, Westminster, Md., The Newman Bookshop, 1934.

Cigno, Giustino, *Giovanni Andrea Serrao e il Giansenismo nell' Italia Meridionale,* Universite de Louvain, Recueil de Travaux 2e Serie, 48e Fascicule, Palermo, Scuola Tipografica F. Istituto d' Assistenzo, 1938.

Clinton, Connell, *The Paschal Precept,* The Catholic University of America Canon Law Studies, n. 73, Washington, D.C., The Catholic University of America, 1932.

Corblet, Jules, *Histoire du Sacrement de l'Eucharistie,* 2 vols., Bruxelles, Societe Generale de Librairie Catholique, 1885.

Coronata, Matthaeus, Conte a, *Institutiones Iuris Canonici ad Usum Utriusque Cleri et Scholarum De Sacramentis Tractus Canonicus,* 3 vols., Romae, Marietti, 1943-1946. Vol. I, 1943.

Dalgairns, J. D., *The Holy Communion, its Philosophy, Theology and Practice,* 6. ed., Dublin, James Duffy & Co. Ltd., 1897.

De Lugo, Joannes Cardinalis, *Disputationes Scholasticae et Morales,* ed. nova, accurante J. B. Fournials, 8 vols., Parisiis, 1868-1891.

Diekamp, Franz, *Katholische Dogmatik,* 3 vols., 7. and 8. eds., Münster, Aschendorff, 1934-1937.

Durieux, P., *The Eucharist, Law and Practice,* translated from the French by Rev. Oliver Dolphin, Chicago, The Lakeside Press, 1926.

Ferreres, J. B., *The Decree on Daily Communion: a Historical Sketch and Commentary,* translated from the Spanish by H. Jimenez, S.J., St. Louis, Herder, 1909.

Frassinetti, Joseph, *The New Parish Priest's Manual,* translation from the Italian by William Hutch, D.D., 2. ed., London, Burns & Oates, 1885.

———— *Compendio della Theologia Morale de S. Alfonso,* 2 vols., Genova, 1866.

Gasparri, Petrus, *Tractatus Canonicus de Sanctissima Eucharistia,* 2 vols., Paris. Delhomme et Briguet, 1897.

Gury, J. P., *Compendium Theologiae Moralis,* ed. Romana, Romae, 1873.

Hedley, J. C., *The Holy Eucharist,* New York, Longmans, Green & Co., 1907.

Hinschius, Paulus, *Decretales Pseudo-Isidorianae et Capitula Angilramni,* Lipsiae, 1863.

Jansenius, Cornelius, *Augustinus,* 3 vols., Lovanii, 1640.

Jorio, Domenico, *La Comunione agl' Infermi, Note Pratiche di Disciplina Sacramentale,* Romae, Pustet, 1931.

Lehmkuhl, A., *Theologia Moralis,* 2 vols., Friburgi Brisgoviae, Herder, 1883-1884.

Liguori, St. Alphonsus, *Homo Apostolicus.* ed. emendatissima, Augustae Taurinorum, Marietti, 1870.

———— *Praxis Confessarii ad bene Excipiendas Confessiones,* Parisiis, apud a Leclere, 1804.

———— *Theologia Moralis,* 9 vols., Taurini, Marietti, 1827.

Lintelo, Jules, *The Eucharistic Triduum, an aid to priests in preaching frequent and daily Communion according to the Decrees of H. H. Pius X,* translated from the French (2. ed.) by F. N. de Zulueta, S.J., Westmonasterii, 1909.

McCormick, Robert Emmet, *Confessors of Religious,* The Catholic University of America Canon Law Studies, n. 33, Washington, D.C., The Catholic University of America, 1926.

Migne, *Patrologiae Cursus Completus, Series Graeca,* 161 vols., Parisiis, 1844-1864.

———— *Patrologiae Cursus Completus, Series Latina,* 221 vols., Parisiis, 1844-1864.

O'Kane, James, *Notes on the Rubrics of the Roman Ritual,* new edition completely revised in accordance with the latest (1925) *editio typica* of the *Rituale Romanum,* and Decrees of the Sacred Congregations by the Rev.

Michael J. Fallon, D.C.L. Dean, St. Patrick's College, Maynooth. Dublin, James Duffy & Co. Ltd., 1938.

Reilly, Edward M., *The General Norms of Dispensation,* The Catholic University of America Canon Law Studies, n. 119, Washington, D.C., The Catholic University of America Press, 1939.

Rosset, M., *Theologia Dogmatica-Moralis, De Sanctissimo et Divinissimo Eucharistiae Mysterio,* Camberii, Chatelain, 1876.

Rufinus, *Die Summa Decretorum der Magister Rufinus,* ed. H. Singer, Paderborn, 1902.

Sabetti, A., *Compendium Theologiae Moralis,* 3. ed., New York, Pustet, 1888.

Scavini, P., *Theologia Moralis Universa,* 11. ed., 4 vols., Mediolani, 1869.

Schaefer, P. Timotheus, *De Religiosis ad Normam Codicis Iuris Canonici,* 3. ed., Romae, S.A.L.E.R. Rappresentante della casa editrice Herder, 1940.

Suarez, F., *Opera Omnia,* 26 vols. in 28, editio nova a Carolo Berton, Paris, Apud Ludovicum Vives, 1856-1868.

Thomas Aquinas, St., *Summa Theologica,* 3. ed., Eminentissimo Cardinali Josepho Pecci oblata, 5 vols., Parisiis, Sumptibus P. Lethielleux, 1886.

——— ——— ——— 5 vols., diligenter emendata De Rubeis, Billuart et aliorum notis selectis ornata, Taurini, Ex officina libraria Marietti, 1933.

Van Hove, A., *Commentarium Lovaniense in Codicem Iuris Canonici,* Vol. I, Tom. I, *Prolegomena,* 2. ed., Mechliniae, Dessain, 1945.

Vermeersch, A.-Creusen, I., *Epitome Iuris Canonici cum Commentariis ad Scholas et ad Usum Privatum,* 6. ed., Romae, H. Dessain, 1937-1946.

Vermeersch, A., *Theologiae Moralis, Principia, Responsa, Consilia,* 4 vols., Brugis, Charles Bayaert, 1927-1933. Vol. I, 3. ed., 1933; Vol. II, 2. ed., 1928; Vol. III, 2. ed., 1927; Vol. IV, 3. ed., 1933.

PERIODICALS

Analecta Iuris Pontificii, Romae, 1855-1869; Parisiis, 1872-1891.

Emmanuel, New York, 1895—.

Recherches de Science Religieuse, Paris, 1910—.

Revue Eucharistique du Clerge, Montreal, 1897—.

The American Ecclesiastical Review (*The Ecclesiastical Review,* from July, 1906—December, 1943) Philadelphia, 1889-1943; Washington, D.C., 1944—.

The Clergy Review, London, 1931—.

The Irish Ecclesiastical Record, Dublin, 1864—.

The Jurist, Washington, D.C., 1941—.

Theological Studies, Baltimore, Md., 1942—.

PRINCIPAL ARTICLES

Alfred, Father, "Some Landmarks of Jansenism"—*The Irish Ecclesiastical Record,* 5th series, V (1915), 449-459.

Anonymous, "De la Frequente Communion"—*Analecta Iuris Pontificii,* VII (1864), 782-847.

Brucker, Joseph, "Saint-Cyran d'apres ses lettres inedites (Manuscrit de Munich)"—*Recherches de science religieuse,* IV (1913), 366—.

Dooley, Eugene, "Priests in the Confessional"—*The Ecclesiastical Review,* CIX (1943), 366-373.

Janssens, Canon, "Masses for Children"—*Emmanuel,* XX (1914), 29-35, 45-52, 106-112, 123-127.

Loyola, Mother Mary, "The Preparation of Children for First Holy Communion"—*Emmanuel,* XX (1914), 213-217.

Mahoney, E. J., "Questions and Answers"—*The Clergy Review,* XXII (1942), 560-561.

Roy, Moise, "Dispense quotidienne du jeune eucharistique dans les hopitaux du Canada"—*Revue Eucharistique du Clerge,* XLVII (1944), 87-93.

———— "Jeune eucharistique mitige pour les infirmiers et les gardes—malades de nuit dans les hopitaux," *Revue Eucharistique du Clerge,* XLIX (1946), 435-437.

———— "Nouvelles dispenses du jeune eucharistique dans les hopitaux du Canada"—Revue Eucharistique du Clerge, XLIX (1946), 432-435.

Werts, Hilary R., "Insuperable Embarrassment and Confession"—*Theological Studies,* IV (1943), 511-524.

ALPHABETICAL INDEX

BIOGRAPHICAL NOTE

Joseph Nicholas Stadler was born at Faribault, Minnesota, on February 13, 1918. He received his elementary education at the Public Schools of La Mesa, California, and San Jacinto, California. In September, 1932 he entered Los Angeles College, the preparatory seminary for the Archdiocese of Los Angeles. On graduation from Los Angeles College in 1938 he entered the North American College, Rome. Having completed his studies in Philosophy at the Pontifical Gregorian University, he returned to the United States because of international complications and the imminence of war. He made his theological studies at St. John's Seminary, Camarillo, California. On May 29, 1944 he was ordained to the priesthood in San Diego, California. In September of the same year he entered the Graduate School of Canon Law of the Catholic University of America. He received the degree of Bachelor of Canon Law in May, 1945, and the degree of Licentiate in Canon Law in June, 1946.

CANON LAW STUDIES *

1. FRERIKS, REV. CELESTINE A., C.PP.S., J.C.D., Religious Congregations in Their External Relations, 121 pp., 1916.
2. GALLIHER, REV. DANIEL M., O.P., J.C.D., Canonical Elections, 117 pp., 1917.
3. BORKOWSKI, REV. AURELIUS L., O.F.M., J.C.D., De Confraternitalibus Ecclesiasticis, 136 pp., 1918.
4. CASTILLO, REV. CAYO, J.C.D., Disertacion Historico-Canonica sobre la Potestad del Cabildo en Sede Vacante o Impedida del Vicario Capitular, 99 pp., 1919 (1918).
5. KUBELBECK, REV. WILLIAM J., S.T.B., J.C.D., The Sacred Penitentiaria and Its Relation to Faculties of Ordinaries and Priests, 129 pp., 1918.
6. PETROVITS, REV. JOSEPH, J.C., S.T.D., J.C.D., The New Church Law on Matrimony, X-461 pp., 1919.
7. HICKEY, REV. JOHN J., S.T.B., J.C.D., Irregularities and Simple Impediments in the New Code of Canon Law, 100 pp., 1920.
8. KLEKOTKA, REV. PETER J., S.T.B., J.C.D., Diocesan Consultors, 179 pp., 1920.
9. WANENMACHER, REV. FRANCIS, J.C.D., The Evidence in Ecclesiastical Procedure Affecting the Marriage Bond, 1920 (Printed 1935).
10. GOLDEN, REV. HENRY FRANCIS, J.C.D., Parochial Benefices in the New Code, IV-119 pp., 1921 (Printed 1925).
11. KOUDELKA, REV. CHARLES J., J.C.D., Pastors, Their Rights and Duties According to the New Code of Canon Law, 211 pp., 1921.
12. MELO, REV. ANTONIUS, O.F.M., J.C.D., De Exemptione Regularium, X-188 pp., 1921.
13. SCHAAF, REV. VALENTINE THEODORE, O.F.M., S.T.B., J.C.D., The Cloister, X-180 pp., 1921.
14. BURKE, REV. THOMAS JOSEPH, S.T.D., J.C.D., Competence in Ecclesiastical Tribunals, IV-117 pp., 1922.
15. LEECH, REV. GEORGE LEO, J.C.D., A Comparative Study of the Constitution "Apostolicae Sedis" and the "Codex Juris Canonici," 179 pp., 1922.
16. MOTRY, REV. HUBERT LOUIS, S.T.D., J.C.D., Diocesan Faculties According to the Code of Canon Law, II-167 pp., 1922.
17. MURPHY, REV. GEORGE LAWRENCE, J.C.D., Delinquencies and Penalties in the Administration and the Reception of the Sacraments, IV-121 pp., 1923.
18. O'REILLY, REV. JOHN ANTHONY, S.T.B., J.C.D., Ecclesiastical Sepulture in the New Code of Canon Law, II-129 pp., 1923.

---

* From nn. 1-100 inclusive only n. 25 is still obtainable.

From n. 101 onward all numbers are available except the following: nn. 101-114 inclusive, and also nn. 116, 118, 120, 122, 123 and 162.

19. MICHALICKA, REV. WENCESLAS CYRILL, O.S.B., J.C.D., Judicial Procedure in Dismissal of Clerical Exempt Religious, 107 pp., 1923.
20. DARGIN, REV. EDWARD VINCENT, S.T.B., J.C.D., Reserved Cases According to the Code of Canon Law, IV-103 pp., 1924.
21. GODFREY, REV. JOHN A., S.T.B., J.C.D., The Right of Patronage According to the Code of Canon Law, 153 pp., 1924.
22. HAGEDORN, REV. FRANCIS EDWARD, J.C.D., General Legislation on Indulgences, II-154 pp., 1924.
23. KING, REV. JAMES IGNATIUS, J.C.D., The Administration of the Sacraments to Dying Non-Catholics, V-141 pp., 1924.
24. WINSLOW, REV. FRANCIS JOSEPH, O.F.M., J.C.D., Vicars and Prefects Apostolic, IV-149 pp., 1924.
25. CORREA, REV. JOSE SERVELION, S.T.L., J.C.D., La Potestad Legislativa de la Iglesia Catolica, IV-127 pp., 1925.
26. DUGAN, REV. HENRY FRANCIS, A.M., J.C.D., The Judiciary Department of the Diocesan Curia, 87 pp., 1925.
27. KELLER, REV. CHARLES FREDERICK, S.T.B., J.C.D., Mass Stipends, 167 pp., 1925.
28. PASCHANG, REV. JOHN LINUS, J.C.D., The Sacramentals According to the Code of Canon Law, 129 pp., 1925.
29. PIONTEK, REV. CYRILLUS, O.F.M., S.T.B., J.C.D., De Indulto Exclaustrationis necnon Saecularizationis, XIII-289 pp., 1925.
30. KEARNEY, REV. RICHARD JOSEPH, S.T.B., J.C.D., Sponsors at Baptism According to the Code of Canon Law, IV-127 pp., 1925.
31. BARTLETT, REV. CHESTER JOSEPH, A.M., LL.B., J.C.D., The Tenure of Parochial Property in the United States of America, V-108 pp., 1926.
32. KILKER, REV. ADRIAN JEROME, J.C.D., Extreme Unction, V-425 pp., 1926.
33. MCCORMICK, REV. ROBERT EMMETT, J.C.D., Confessors of Religious, VIII-266 pp., 1926.
34. MILLER, REV. NEWTON THOMAS, J.C.D., Founded Masses According to the Code of Canon Law, VII-93 pp., 1926.
35. ROELKER, REV. EDWARD G., S.T.D., J.C.D., Principles of Privilege According to the Code of Canon Law, XI-166 pp., 1926.
36. BAKALARCZYK, REV. RICHARDUS, M.I.C., J.U.D., De Novitiatu. VIII-208 pp., 1927.
37. PIZZUTI, REV. LAWRENCE, O.F.M., J.U.L., De Parochis Religiosis, 1927. (Not Printed.)
38. BLILEY, REV. NICHOLAS MARTIN, O.S.B., J.C.D., Altars According to the Code of Canon Law, XIX-132 pp., 1927.
39. BROWN, MR. BRENDAN FRANCIS, A.B., LL.M., J.U.D., The Canonical Juristic Personality with Special References to its Status in the United States of America, V-212 pp., 1927.
40. CAVANAUGH, REV. WILLIAM THOMAS, C.P., J.U.D., The Reservation of the Blessed Sacrament, VIII-101 pp., 1927.

41. DOHENY, REV. WILLIAM J., C.S.C., A.B., J.U.D., Church Property: Modes Acquisition, X-118 pp., 1927.
42. FELDHAUS, REV. ALOYSIUS H., C.PP.S., J.C.D., Oratories, IX-141 pp., 1927.
43. KELLY, REV. JAMES PATRICK, A.B., J.C.D., The Jurisdiction of the Simple Confessor, X-208 pp., 1927.
44. NEUBERGER, REV. NICHOLAS J., J.C.D., Canon 6 or the Relation of the Codex Juris Canonici to the Preceding Legislation, V-95 pp., 1927.
45. O'KEEFE, REV. GERALD MICHAEL, J.C.D., Matrimonial Dispensations, Powers of Bishops, Priests, and Confessors, VIII-232 pp., 1927.
46. QUIGLEY, REV. JOSEPH A. M., A.B., J.C.D., Condemned Societies, 139 pp., 1927.
47. ZAPLOTNIK, REV. JOHANNES LEO, J.C.D., De Vicariis Foraneis, X-142 pp., 1927.
48. DUSKIE, REV. JOHN ALOYSIUS, A.B., J.C.D., The Canonical Status of the Orientals in the United States, VIII-196 pp., 1928.
49. HYLAND, REV. FRANCIS EDWARD, J.C.D., Excommunication, Its Nature, Historical Development and Effects, VIII-181 pp., 1928.
50. REINMANN, REV. GERALD JOSEPH, O.M.C., J.C.D., The Third Order Secular of Saint Francis, 201 pp., 1928.
51. SCHENK, REV. FRANCIS J., J.C.D., The Matrimonial Impediments of Mixed Religion and Disparity of Cult, XVI-318 pp., 1929.
52. COADY, REV. JOHN JOSEPH, S.T.D., J.U.D., A.M., The Appointment of Pastors, VIII-150 pp., 1929.
53. KAY, REV. THOMAS HENRY, J.C.D., Competence in Matrimonial Procedure, VIII-164 pp., 1929.
54. TURNER, REV. SIDNEY JOSEPH, C.P., J.U.D., The Vow of Poverty, XLIX-217 pp., 1929.
55. KEARNEY, REV. RAYMOND A., A.B., S.T.D., J.C.D., The Principles of Delegation, VII-149 pp., 1929.
56. CONRAN, REV. EDWARD JAMES, A.B., J.C.D., The Interdict, V-163 pp., 1930.
57. O'NEILL, REV. WILLIAM H., J.C.D., Papal Rescripts of Favor, VII-218 pp., 1930.
58. BASTNAGEL, REV. CLEMENT VINCENT, J.U.D., The Appointment of Parochial Adjutants and Assistants, XV-257 pp., 1930.
59. FERRY, REV. WILLIAM A., A.B., J.C.D., Stole Fees, V-136 pp., 1930.
60. COSTELLO, REV. JOHN MICHAEL, A.B., J.C.D., Domicile and Quasi-Domicile, VII-201 pp., 1930.
61. KREMER, REV. MICHAEL NICHOLAS, A.B., S.T.B., J.C.D., Church Support in the United States, VI-136 pp., 1930.
62. ANGULO, REV. LUIS, C.M., J.C.D., Legislation de la Iglesia sobre la intencion en la application de la Santa Misa, VII-104 pp., 1931.
63. FREY, REV. WOLFGANG NORBERT, O.S.B., A.B., J.C.D., The Act of Religious Profession, VIII-174 pp., 1931.

64. ROBERTS, REV. JAMES BRENDAN, A.B., J.C.D., The Banns of Marriage, XIV-140 pp., 1931.
65. RYDER, REV. RAYMOND ALOYSIUS, A.B., J.C.D., Simony, IX-151 pp., 1931.
66. CAMPAGNA, REV. ANGELO, Ph.D., J.U.D., Il Vicario Generale del Vescovo, VII-205 pp., 1931.
67. COX, REV. JOSEPH GODFREY, A.B., J.C.D., The Administration of Seminaries, VI-124 pp., 1931.
68. GREGORY, REV. DONALD J., J.U.D., The Pauline Privilege, XV-165 pp., 1931.
69. DONOHUE, REV. JOHN F., J.C.D., The Impediment of Crime, VII-110 pp., 1931.
70. DOOLEY, REV. EUGENE A., O.M.I., J.C.D., Church Law on Sacred Relics, IX-143 pp., 1931.
71. ORTH, REV. CLEMENT RAYMOND, O.M.C., J.C.D., The Approbation of Religious Institutes, 171 pp., 1931.
72. PERNICONE, REV. JOSEPH M., A.B., J.C.D., The Ecclesiastical Prohibition of Books, XII-267 pp., 1932.
73. CLINTON, REV. CONNELL, A.B., J.C.D., The Paschal Precept, IX-108 pp., 1932.
74. DONNELLY, REV. FRANCIS B., A.M., S.T.L., J.C.D., The Diocesan Synod, VIII-125 pp., 1932.
75. TORRENTE, REV. CAMILO, C.M.F., J.C.D., Las Procesiones Sagradas, V-145 pp., 1932.
76. MURPHY, REV. EDWIN J., C.PP.S., J.C.D., Suspension Ex Informata Conscientia, XI-122 pp., 1932.
77. MACKENZIE, REV. ERIC F., A.M., S.T.L., J.C.D., The Delict of Heresy in its Commission, Penalization, Absolution, VII-124 pp., 1932.
78. LYONS, REV. AVITUS E., S.T.B., J.C.D., The Collegiate Tribunal of First Instance, XI-147 pp., 1932.
79. CONNOLLY, REV. THOMAS A., J.C.D., Appeals, XI-195, pp. 1932.
80. SANGMEISTER, REV. JOSEPH V., A.B., J.C.D., Force and Fear as Precluding Matrimonial Consent, V-211 pp. 1932.
81. JAEGER, REV. LEO A., A.B., J.C.D., The Administration of Vacant and Quasi-Vacant Episcopal Sees in the United States, IX-229 pp., 1932.
82. RIMLINGER, REV. HERBERT T., J.C.D., Error Invalidating Matrimonial Consent, VII-79 pp., 1932.
83. BARRETT, REV. JOHN D. M., SS., J.C.D., A Comparative Study of the Councils of Baltimore and the Code of Canon Law, X-223 pp., 1932.
84. CARBERRY, REV. JOHN J., Ph.D., S.T.D., J.C.D., The Juridical Form of Marriage, X-177 pp., 1934.
85. DOLAN, REV. JOHN L., A.B., J.C.D., The Defensor Vinculi, XII-157 pp., 1934.
86. HANNAN, REV. JEROME D., A.M., S.T.D., LL.B., J.C.D., The Canon Law of Wills, IX-517 pp., 1934.

87. LEMIEUX, REV. DELISE A., A.M., J.C.D., The Sentence in Ecclesiastical Procedure, IX-131 pp., 1934.
88. O'ROURKE, REV. JAMES J., A.B., J.C.D., Parish Registers, VII-109 pp., 1934.
89. TIMLIN, REV. BARTHOLOMEW, O.F.M., A.M., J.C.D., Conditional Matrimonial Consent, X-381 pp., 1934.
90. WAHL, REV. FRANCIS X., A.B., J.C.D., The Matrimonial Impediments of Consanguinity and Affinity, VI-125 pp., 1934.
91. WHITE, REV. ROBERT J., A.B., LL.B., S.T.B., J.C.D., Canonical Ante-Nuptial Promises and the Civil Law, VI-152 pp., 1934.
92. HERRERA, REV. ANTONIO PARRA, O.C.D., J.C.D., Legislacion Ecclesiastica sobra el Ayuno y la Abstinencia, XI-191 pp., 1935.
93. KENNEDY, REV. EDWIN J., J.C.D., The Special Matrimonial Process in Cases of Evident Nullity, X-165 pp., 1935.
94. MANNING, REV. JOHN J., A.B., J.C.D., Presumption of Law in Matrimonial Procedure, XI-111 pp., 1935.
95. MOEDER, REV. JOHN M., J.C.D., The Proper Bishop for Ordination and Dismissorial Letters, VII-135 pp., 1935.
96. O'MARA, REV. WILLIAM A., A.B., J.C.D., Canonical Causes for Matrimonial Dispensations, IX-155 pp., 1935.
97. REILLY, REV. PETER, J.C.D., Residence of Pastors, IX-81 pp., 1935.
98. SMITH, REV. MARINER T., O.P., S.T. Lr., J.C.D., The Penal Law for Religious, VIII-169 pp., 1935.
99. WHALEN, REV. DONALD W., A.M., J.C.D., The Value of Testimonial Evidence in Matrimonial Procedure, XIII-297 pp., 1935.
100. CLEARY, REV. JOSEPH F., J.C.D., Canonical Limitations on the Alienation of Church Property, VIII-141 pp., 1936.
101. GLYNN, REV. JOHN C., J.C.D., The Promoter of Justice, XX-337 pp., 1936.
102. BRENNAN, REV. JAMES H., S.S., M.A., S.T.B., J.C.D., The Simple Convalidation of Marriage, VI-135 pp., 1937.
103. BRUNINI, REV. JOSEPH BERNARD, J.C.D., The Clerical Obligations of Canons 139 and 142, X-121 pp., 1937.
104. CONNOR, REV. MAURICE, A.B., J.C.D., The Administrative Removal of Pastors, VIII-159 pp., 1937.
105. GUILFOYLE, REV. MERLIN JOSEPH, J.C.D., Custom, XI-144 pp., 1937.
106. HUGHES, REV. JAMES AUSTIN, A.B., A.M., J.C.D., Witnesses in Criminal Trials of Clerics, IX-140 pp., 1937.
107. JANSEN, REV. RAYMOND J., A.B., S.T.L., J.C.D., Canonical Provisions for Catechetical Instruction, VII-153 pp., 1937.
108. KEALY, REV. JOHN JAMES, A.B., J.C.D., The Introductory Libellus in Church Court Procedure, XI-121 pp., 1937.
109. MCMANUS, REV. JAMES EDWARD, C.SS.R., J.C.D., The Administration of Temporal Goods in Religious Institutes, XVI-196 pp., 1937.

110. MORIARTY, REV. EUGENE JAMES, J.C.D., Oaths in Ecclesiastical Courts, X-115 pp., 1937.

111. RAINER, REV. ELIGIUS GEORGE, C.SS.R., J.C.D., Suspension of Clerics, XVII-249 pp., 1937.

112. REILLY, REV. THOMAS F., C.SS.R., J.C.D., Visitation of Religious, VI-195 pp., 1938.

113. MORIARTY, REV. FRANCIS E., C.SS.R., J.C.D., The Extraordinary Absolution from Censures, XV-334 pp., 1938.

114. CONNOLLY, REV. NICHOLAS P., J.C.D., The Canonical Erection of Parishes, X-132 pp., 1938.

115. DONOVAN, REV. JAMES JOSEPH, J.C.D., The Pastor's Obligation in Prenuptial Investigation, XII-322 pp., 1938.

116. HARRIGAN, REV. ROBERT J., M.A., S.T.B., J.C.D., The Radical Sanation of Invalid Marriages, VIII-208 pp., 1938.

117. BOFFA, REV. CONRAD HUMBERT, J.C.D., Canonical Provisions for Catholic Schools, VII-211 pp., 1939.

118. PARSONS, REV. ANSCAR JOHN, O.M.Cap., J.C.D., Canonical Elections, XII-236 pp., 1939.

119. REILLY, REV. EDWARD MICHAEL, A.B., J.C.D., The General Norms of Dispensation, XII-156 pp., 1939.

120. RYAN, REV. GERALD ALOYSIUS, A.B., J.C.D., Principles of Episcopal Jurisdiction, XII-172 pp., 1939.

121. BURTON, REV. FRANCIS JAMES, C.S.C., A.B., J.C.D., A Commentary on Canon 1125, X-222 pp., 1940.

122. MIASKIEWICZ, REV. FRANCIS SIGISMUND, J.C.D., Supplied Jurisdiction According to Canon 209, XII-340 pp., 1940.

123. RICE, REV. PATRICK WILLIAM, A.B., J.C.D., Proof of Death in Prenuptial Investigation, VIII-156 pp., 1940.

124. ANGLIN, REV. THOMAS FRANCIS, M.S., J.C.D., The Eucharistic Fast, VIII-183 pp., 1941.

125. COLEMAN, REV. JOHN JEROME, J.C.D., The Minister of Confirmation, VI-153 pp., 1941.

126. DOWNS, REV. JOHN EMMANUEL, A.B., J.C.D., The Concept of Clerical Immunity, XI-163 pp., 1941.

127. ESSWEIN, REV ANTHONY ALBERT, J.C.D., Extrajudicial Penal Powers of Ecclesiastical Superiors, X-144 pp., 1941.

128. FARRELL, REV. BENJAMIN FRANCIS, M.A., S.T.L., J.C.D., The Rights and Duties of the Local Ordinary Regarding Congregations of Women Religious of Pontifical Approval, V-195 pp., 1941.

129. FEENEY, REV. THOMAS JOHN, A.B., S.T.L., J.C.D., Restitutio in Integrum, VI-169 pp., 1941.

130. FINDLAY, REV. STEPHEN WILLIAM, O.S.B., A.B., J.C.D., Canonical Norms Governing the Deposition and Degradation of Clerics, XVII-279 pp., 1941.

131. GOODWINE, REV. JOHN, A.B., S.T.L., J.C.D., The Right of the Church to Acquire Property, VIII-119 pp., 1941.
132. HESTON, REV. EDWARD LOUIS, C.S.C., Ph.D., S.T.D., J.C.D., The Alienation of Church Property in the United States, XII-222 pp., 1941.
133. HOGAN, REV. JAMES JOHN, A.B., S.T.L., J.C.D., Judicial Advocates and Procurators, XIII-200 pp., 1941.
134. KEALY, REV. THOMAS M., A.B., Litt.B., J.C.D., Dowry of Women Religious, IX-152 pp., 1941.
135. KEENE, REV. MICHAEL JAMES, O.S.B., J.C.D., Religious Ordinaries and Canon 198, V-164 pp., 1942.
136. KERIN, REV. CHARLES A., S.S., M.A., S.T.B., J.C.D., The Privation of Christian Burial, XVI-279 pp., 1941.
137. LOUIS, REV. WILLIAM FRANCIS, M.A., J.C.D., Diocesan Archives, X-101 pp., 1941.
138. MCDEVITT, REV. GILBERT JOSEPH, A.B., J.C.D., Legitimacy and Legitimation, X-247 pp., 1941.
139. MCDONOUGH, REV. THOMAS JOSEPH, A.B., J.C.D., Apostolic Administrators, X-217 pp., 1941.
140. MEIER, REV. CARL ANTHONY, A.B., J.C.D., Penal Administrative Procedure Against Negligent Pastors, XI-240 pp., 1941.
141. SCHMIDT, REV. JOHN ROGG, A.B., J.C.D., The Principles of Authentic Interpretation in Canon 17 of the Code of Canon Law, XII-331 pp., 1941.
142. SLAFKOSKY, REV. ANDREW LEONARD, A.B., J.C.D., The Canonical Episcopal Visitation of the Diocese, X-197 pp., 1941.
143. SWOBODA, REV. INNOCENT ROBERT, O.F.M., J.C.D., Ignorance in Relation to the Imputability of Delicts, IX-271 pp., 1941.
144. DUBE, REV. ARTHUR JOSEPH, A.B., J.C.D., The General Principles for the Reckoning of Time in Canon Law, VIII-299 pp., 1941.
145. MCBRIDE, REV. JAMES T., A.B., J.C.D., Incardination and Excardination of Seculars, XX-585 pp., 1941.
146. KROL, REV. JOHN T., J.C.D., The Defendant in Ecclesiastical Trials, XII-207 pp., 1942.
147. COMYNS, REV. JOSEPH J., C.SS.R., A.B., J.C.D., Papal and Episcopal Administration of Church Property, XIV-155 pp., 1942.
148. BARRY, REV. GARRETT FRANCIS, O.M.I., J.C.D., Violation of the Cloister, XII-260 pp., 1942.
149. BOLDUC, REV. GATIEN, C.S.V., A.B., S.T.L., J.C.D., Les Etudes dans les Religions Cléricales, VIII-155 pp., 1942.
150. BOYLE, REV. DAVID JOHN, M.A., J.C.D., The Juridic Effects of Moral Certitude on Pre-Nuptial Guarantees, XII-188 pp., 1942.
151. CANAVAN, REV. WALTER JOSEPH, M.A., Litt.D., J.C.D., The Profession of Faith, XII-143 pp., 1942.
152. DESROCHERS, REV. BRUNO, A.B., Ph.L., S.T.B., J.C.D., Le Premier Concile Plénier de Québec et le Code de Droit Canonique, XIV-186 pp., 1942.

153. Dillon, Rev. Robert Edward, A.B., J.C.D., Common Law Marriage, X-148 pp., 1942.
154. Dodwell, Rev. Edward John, Ph.D., S.T.B., J.C.D., The Time and Place for the Celebration of Marriage, X-156 pp., 1942.
155. Donnellan, Rev. Thomas Andrew, A.B., J.C.D., The Obligation of the Missa pro Populo, VII-131 pp., 1942.
156 Eltz, Rev. Louis Anthony, A.B., J.C.D., Cooperation in Crime, XII-208 pp., 1942.
157. Gass, Rev. Sylvester Francis, M.A., J.C.D., Ecclesiastical Pensions, XI-206 pp., 1942.
158. Guiniven, Rev. John Joseph, C.SS.R., J.C.D., The Precept of Hearing Mass, XIV-188 pp., 1942.
159. Gulczynski, Rev. John Theophilus, J.C.D., The Desecration and Violation of Churches, X-126 pp., 1942.
160. Hammill, Rev. John Leo, M.A., J.C.D., The Obligations of the Traveler According to Canon 14, VIII-204 pp., 1942.
161. Haydt, Rev. John Joseph, A.B., J.C.D., Reserved Benefices, XI-148 pp., 1942.
162. Huser, Rev. Roger John, O.F.M., A.B., J.C.D., The Crime of Abortion in Canon Law, XII-187 pp., 1942.
163. Kearney, Rev. Francis Patrick, A.B., S.T.L., J.C.D., The Principles of Canon 1127, X-162 pp., 1942.
164. Linahen, Rev. Leo James, S.T.L., J.C.D., De Absolutione, Complicis in Peccato Turpi, V-114 pp., 1942.
165. McCloskey, Rev. Joseph Aloysius, A.B., J.C.D., The Subject of Ecclesiastical Law According to Canon 12, XVII-246 pp., 1942.
166. O'Neill, Rev. Francis Joseph, C.SS.R., J.C.D., The Dismissal of Religious in Temporary Vows, VIII-220 pp., 1942.
167. Prince, Rev. John Edward, A.B., S.T.B., J.C.D., The Diocesan Chancellor, X-136 pp., 1942.
168. Riesner, Rev. Albert Joseph, C.SS.R., J.C.D., Apostates and Fugitives from Religious Institutes, IX-168 pp., 1942.
169. Stenger, Rev. Joseph Bernard, J.C.D., The Moragaging of Church Property, 186 pp., 1942.
170. Waldron, Rev. Joseph Francis, A.B., J.C.D., The Minister of Baptism, XII-197 pp., 1942.
171. Willett, Rev. Robert Albert, J.C.D., The Probative Value of Documents in Ecclesiastical Trials, X-124 pp., 1942.
172. Woeber, Rev. Edward Martin, M.A., J.C.D., The Interpellations, XII-161 pp., 1942.
173. Benko, Rev. Matthew Aloysius, O.S.B., M.A., J.C.D., The Abbot *Nullius*, XVI-148 pp., 1943.
174. Christ, Rev. Joseph James, M.A., S.T.L., J.C.D., Dispensation from Vindicative Penalties, XIV-285 pp., 1943.

175. Clancy, Rev. Patrick M. J., O.P., A.B., S.T.Lr., J.C.D., The Local Religious Superior, X-229 pp., 1943.

176. Clarke, Rev. Thomas James, J.C.D., Parish Societies, XII-147 pp., 1943.

177. Connolly, Rev. John Patrick, S.T.L., J.C.D., Synodal Examiners and Parish Priest Consultors, X-223 pp., 1943.

178. Drumm, Rev. William Martin, A.B., J.C.D., Hospital Chaplains, XII-175 pp., 1943.

179. Flanagan, Rev. Bernard Joseph, A.B., S.T.L., J.C.D., The Canonical Erection of Religious Houses, X-147 pp., 1943.

180. Kelleher, Rev. Stephen Joseph, A.B., S.T.B., J.C.D., Discussions with Non-Catholics: Canonical Legislation, X-93 pp., 1943.

181. Lewis, Rev. Gordian, C.P. J.C.D., Chapters in Religious Institutes, XII-169 pp., 1943.

182. Marx, Rev. Adolph, J.C.D., The Declaration of Nullity of Marriages Contracted Outside the Church, X-151 pp., 1943.

183. Matulenas, Rev. Raymond Anthony, O.S.B., A.B., J.C.D., Communication, a Source of Privileges, XII-225 pp., 1943.

184. O'Leary, Rev. Charles Gerard, C.SS.R., J.C.D., Religious Dismissed After Perpetual Profession, X-213 pp., 1943.

185. Power, Rev. Cornelius Michael, J.C.D., The Blessing of Cemeteries, XII-231 pp., 1943.

186. Shuhler, Rev. Ralph Vincent, O.S.A., J.C.D., Privileges of Religious to Absolve and Dispense, XII-195 pp., 1943.

187. Ziolkowski, Rev. Thaddeus Stanislaus, A.B., J.C.D., The Consecration and Blessing of Churches, XII-151 pp., 1943.

188. Heneghan, Rev. John Joseph, S.T.D., J.C.D., The Marriages of Unworthy Catholics: Canons 1065 and 1066, XVI-213 pp., 1944.

189. Carroll, Rev. Coleman Francis, M.A., S.T.L., J.C.L., Charitable Institutions.

190. Ciesluk, Rev. Joseph Edward, Ph.B., S.T.L., J.C.L., National Parishes in the United States.

191. Coburn, Rev. Vincent Paul, A.B., J.C.D., Marriages of Conscience, XII-172 pp., 1944.

192. Connors, Rev. Charles Paul, C.S.Sp., A.B., J.C.D., Extra-Judicial Procurators in the Code of Canon Law, X-94 pp., 1944.

193. Coyle, Rev. Paul Raymond, A.B., J.C.D., Judicial Exceptions, X-142 pp., 1944.

194. Fair, Rev. Bartholomew Francis, A.B., S.T.L., J.C.D., The Impediment of Abduction, XII-122 pp., 1944.

195. Gallagher, Rev. Thomas Raphael, O.P., A.B., S.T.Lr., J.C.D., The Examination of the Qualities of the Ordinand, X-166 pp., 1944.

196. Gannon, Rev. John Mark, S.T.L., J.C.D., The Interstices Required for the Promotion to Orders, XII-100 pp., 1944.

197. Goldsmith, Rev. J. William, B.C.S., S.T.L., J.C.D., The Competence of Church and State Over Marriages—Disputed Points, X-128 pp., 1944.
198. Goodwine, Rev. Joseph Gerard, A.B., S.T.B., J.C.D., The Reception of Converts, XIV-326 pp., 1944.
199. Kowalski, Rev. Romuald Eugene, O.F.M., A.B., J.C.D., Sustenance of Religious Houses of Regulars, X-174 pp., 1944.
200. McCoy, Rev. Alan Edward, O.F.M.; J.C.D., Force and Fear in Relation to Delictual Imputability and Penal Responsibility, XII-160 pp., 1944.
201. McDevitt, Rev. Vincent John, Ph.B., S.T.L., J.C.L., Perjury.
202. Martin, Rev. Thomas Owen, Ph.D., S.T.D., J.C.D., Adverse Possession, Prescription and Limitation of Actions: The Canonical "Praescriptio," XX-208 pp., 1944.
203. Miklosovic, Rev. Paul John, A.B., J.C.L., Attempted Marriages and Their Consequent Juridic Effects.
204. Mundy, Rev. Thomas Maurice, A.B., S.T.L., J.C.D., The Union of Parishes, X-164 pp., 1944.
205. O'Dea, Rev. John Coyle, A.B., J.C.D., The Matrimonial Impediment of Nonage, VIII-126 pp., 1944.
206. Olalia, Rev. Alexander Ayson, S.T.L., J.C.D., A Comparative Study of the Christian Constitution of States and the Constitution of the Philippine Commonwealth, XII-136 pp., 1944.
207. Poisson, Rev. Pierre-Marie, C.S.C., A.B., Ph.L., Th.L., J.C.L., Droits Patrimoniaux des Maisons et des Eglises Religieuses.
208. Stadalnikas, Rev. Casimir Joseph, M.I.C., J.C.D., Reservation of Censures, X-141 pp., 1944.
209. Sullivan, Rev. Eugene Henry, S.T.L., J.C.D., Proof of the Reception of the Sacraments, X-165 pp., 1944.
210. Vaughan, Rev. William Edward, J.C.D., Constitutions for Diocesan Courts, X-210 pp., 1944.
211. Paro, Rev. Gino, S.T.D., J.C.L., The Right of Apostolic Legation.
212. Balzer, Rev. Ralph Francis, C.P., J.C.D., The Computation of Time in a Canonical Novitiate, X-227 pp., 1945.
213. Dougherty, Rev. John Whelan, A.B., S.T.L., J.C.D., De Inquisitione Speciali, XII-195 pp., 1945.
214. Dziob, Rev. Michael Walter, J.C.D., The Sacred Congregation for the Oriental Church, XII-181 pp., 1945.
215. Eidenschink, Rev. John Albert, O.S.B., B.A., J.C.D., The Election of Bishops in the Letters of Pope Gregory the Great, VIII-200 pp., 1945.
216. Gill, Rev. Nicholas, C.P., J.C.D., The Spiritual Prefect in Clerical Religious Houses of Study, X-140 pp., 1945.
217. Hynes, Rev. Harry Gerard, S.T.L., J.C.D., The Privileges of Cardinals, XII-183 pp., 1945.
218. McDevitt, Rev. Gerald Vincent, S.T.L., J.C.D., The Renunciation of an Ecclesiastical Office, XIV-179 pp., 1945.

219. MANNING, REV. JOSEPH LEROY, J.C.D., The Free Conferral of Offices, VII-116 pp., 1945.
220. MEYER, REV. LOUIS G., O.S.B., A.B., S.T.B., J.C.D., Alms-gathering by Religious, XII-163 pp., 1945.
221. O'DONNELL, REV. CLETUS FRANCIS, M.A., J.C.D., The Marriage of Minors, XII-268 pp., 1945.
222. PRUNSKIS, REV. JOSEPH, J.C.D., Comparative Law, Ecclesiastical and Civil, in Lithuanian Concordat, X-161 pp., 1945.
223. SWEENEY, REV. FRANCIS PATRICK, C.SS.R., J.C.D., The Reduction of Clerics to the Lay State, X-199 pp., 1945.
224. VOGELPOHL, REV. HENRY JOHN, J.C.D., The Simple Impediments to Holy Orders, XVI-190 pp., 1945.
225. BROCKHAUS, REV. THOMAS AQUINAS, O.S.B., J.C.D., Religious who are known as *Conversi,* X-127 pp., 1945.
226. GRIESE, REV. ORVILLE NICHOLAS, S.T.D., J.C.D., Marriage and the Procreation of Offspring, XVI-224 pp., 1945.
227. BOUDREAUX, REV. WARREN LOUIS, J.C.L., The *"ab acatholicis nati"* of Canon 1099, § 2.
228. BOWE, REV. THOMAS JOSEPH, A.B., J.C.L., Religious Superioresses.
229. DIEDERICHS, REV. MICHAEL FERDINAND, S.C.J., J.C.D., The Jurisdiction of the Latin Ordinaries over their Oriental Subjects, XIV-153 pp., 1946.
230. DINGMAN, REV. MAURICE JOHN, A.B., S.T.L., J.C.L., The Plaintiff in Contentious Trials.
231. FRISON, REV. BASIL, C.M.F., M.MUS., J.C.D., The Retroactivity of Law, X-221 pp., 1946.
232. GALVIN, REV. WILLIAM ANTHONY, M.A., J.C.D., The Administrative Transfer of Pastors, XII-288 pp., 1946.
233. GORACY, REV. JOSEPH C., J.C.L., The Diriment Matrimonial Impediment of Major Orders.
234. HALE, REV. JOSEPH FRANCIS, M.A., S.T.L., J.C.L., The Pastor of Burial.
235. HENRY, REV. JOSEPH ARTHUR, A.B., J.C.D., The Mass and Holy Communion: Interritual Law, XII-138 pp., 1946.
236. LINENBERGER, REV. HERBERT, C.PP.S., J.C.L., The False Denunciation of an Innocent Confessor.
237. LOWRY, REV. JAMES MARTIN, A.B., J.C.D., Dispensation from Private Vows, XII-216 pp., 1946.
238. LYNCH, REV. GEORGE EDWARD, A.B., S.T.L., J.C.D., Coadjutors and Auxiliaries of Bishops, X-107 pp., 1947.
239. LYNCH, REV. TIMOTHY, M.S.SS.T., J.C.D., Contracts between Bishops and Religious Congregations, XIII-232 pp., 1946.
240. MCCLUNN, REV. JUSTIN DAVID, A.B., S.T.L., J.C.D., Administrative Recourse, VII-142 pp., 1946.
241. LOHMULLER, REV. MARTIN NICHOLAS, A.B., J.C.D., The Promulgation of Law, XII-140 pp., 1947.

242. McGrath, Rev. James, A.B., J.C.D., The Privilege of the Canon, XII-156 pp., 1946.

243. Marbach, Rev. Joseph Francis, A.B., J.C.D., Marriage Legislation for the Catholics of the Oriental Rites in the United States and Canada, XIV-344 pp., 1946.

244. Shimkus, Rev. Bernard Aloysius, A.B., J.C.L., The Determination and Transfer of Rite.

245. Smith, Rev. Vincent Michael, A.B., S.T.L., J.C.L., Ignorance Affecting Matrimonial Consent.

246. Wachtrle, Rev. Paul Anthony, A.B., J.C.L., The Baptism of the Children of Non-Catholics.

247. Crotty, Rev. Matthew M., J.C.L., The Recipient of First Holy Communion.

248. Eagleton, Rev. George, J.C.L. The Quinquennial Faculties, Formula IV.

249. Gibbons, Rev. Marion L., C.M., LL.B., J.C.L., Domicile of the Wife Unlawfully Separated from Her Husband.

250. Kelly, Rev. Bernard M., S.T.L., J.C.L., The Functions Reserved to Pastors.

251. Kilcullen, Rev. Thomas J., LL.M., J.C.L., The Collegiate Moral Person as Party Litigant.

252. Lafontaine, Rev. Germain J., W.F., J.C.L., Relations Canoniques entre Le Missionnaire et Ses Superieurs.

253. Lane, Rev. Loras T., A.B., S.T.L., J.C.L., Matrimonial Procedure in the Ordinary Court of Second Instance.

254. Lover, Rev. James F., C.SS.R., J.C.L., The Master of Novices.

255. McNicholas, Rev. Timothy J., J.C.L., The *Septimae Manus* Witness.

256. Marositz, Rev. Joseph J., M.S.C., J.C.L., Obligations and Privileges of Religious Promoted to the Episcopal or Cardinalitial Dignities.

257. Murphy, Rev. Francis J., A.B., J.C.L., Legislative Powers of the Provincial Council.

258. O'Brien, Rev. Romaeus W., O. Carm., J.C.L., The Provincial Superior in Religious Orders of Men.

259. Pfaller, Rev. Benedict A., O.S.B., J.C.L., The *Ipso facto* Effected Dismissal of Religious.

260. Popek, Rev. Alphonse S., M.A., J.C.L., The Rights and Obligations of Metropolitans.

261. Ristuccia, Rev. Bernard J., C.M., J.C.L., Quasi-Religious.

262. Sonntag, Rev. Nathaniel L., O.F.M., Cap., J.C.L., Censorship of Special Classes of Books.

263. Stadler, Rev. Joseph N., J.C.L., Frequent Holy Communion.

264. Szal, Rev. Ignatius J., J.C.L., The Communication of Catholics with Schismatics.

265. Wagner, Rev. Urban S., O.F.M., Conv., J.C.L., Parochial Substitute Vicars and Supplying Priests.

www.ingramcontent.com/pod-product-compliance
Lightning Source LLC
LaVergne TN
LVHW050225080826

844660LV00012B/471
9780813224411